# TAKING THE LONG WAY HOME

## Peter Kimber

British Library Cataloguing in Publication Data:
a catalogue record for this publication
is available from the British Library

ISBN: 978-1-912052-76-9

The right of Peter Kimber to be identified as the author of this work
has been asserted by him in accordance with
the Copyright, Designs and Patents Act 1988

Typeset in 11.5 Minion Pro at Haddington, Scotland

Printed by West Port Print, St Andrews

# Contents

# Preface

This is not an auto-biography and indeed I am not sure if it fits any genre. It is a collection of places and faces which helped to make my life interesting and occasionally, frightening. I am an active Christian, but the events and people in this book are offered simply for themselves and with no purpose beyond the telling of some stories.

Passages in italics throughout the book offer additional information about parts of the text and may be read or not, according to the reader's interests. And in an appendix, there is a text of the first climbing of a mountain in Antarctica which may be of interest to a few but probably not many.

All profits from sales will go to Scripture Union.

Old men forget, and all shall be forgot,
But he'll remember, with advantages,
What feats he did that day.

(Shakespeare, *Henry V*)

# Chapter 1   Growing Up

## Early Days (1937 – 1950)

I was born on the 3$^{rd}$ of September 1937, two years before the second world War broke out on the same date. I was born to be a traveller, and a traveller before I was born, since my mother travelled three hundred and fifty miles to give birth to me, from Madras, in South India, to Ootacamund – also known as snooty Ooty – six thousand feet up in the Nilgiri Hills, surrounded by tea plantations. Later I went to school in the same town.

When the second world war was over, in 1945, I went out to India with my parents, living in a big town called Coimbatore, and leaving my older brother and twin sisters in Britain. My school was fifty miles away so I had to be a boarder. For my first term my Dad took me by bus – starting at 5.00 in the morning – to a town called Mettupalayam, (or Metty for short) twenty miles away across flat farm land, where we caught a second bus. The next thirty miles were totally different because the bus had to climb about 5,000 feet through thick jungle for the first part and then through tea plantations higher up, finishing with rolling grasslands which the homesick British called 'The Downs' in memory of the similar hills on the south coast of England. There were more than twenty hairpin bends. The end of the journey was at Ootacamund, or Ooty, for short.

After that first journey, I travelled by myself at the beginning of term at a boarding school, starting at 5am and changing buses at Metty, getting to school for lessons at 9am. It was quite scary the first time, but I got used to it and I am sure that helped to give me confidence and a love of travelling.

There was – and still is – a famous railway line climbing up from Metty to Ooty and periodically the BBC shows films about these famous railways, with the engine at the back of the train, straddling a rack and pinion making a third rail which provides traction and prevents wheels from slipping.

Places like Ooty were called hill stations where people went to avoid the hottest weather in the months of May and June. Breeks School had a prominent place right in the centre of the town, overlooking the junction of the main road from the planes and the commercial area. When I say that junction was called 'Charing Cross', it says a lot about the British presence in India: the superiority of everything British; the nostalgia of tea-planters' wives for 'home', and it gave the idea that for all the two hundred years of British power in India, we would always be leaving soon, if only on furlough.

The school itself was built in red sandstone in a mock-Gothic style. It was originally for the children of missionaries but there were places for local children whose aspiring parents wanted them to have a British education. The teachers were local British people, Anglo-Indians and a few Indians. My resident house-master was John Jacob, an Armenian born and brought up in India. At the time, I knew him as a pleasant, humorous but stern housemaster of indeterminate age. Our lives would cross several times in the future in ways I could never have anticipated. I assumed that he was 'old' without any thought about how old, because teachers are – old. I remember going to a school some miles away to watch an inter-school athletics match. We were short of one runner for the 4x440 yards relay (or 400 metres today). Imagine my astonishment when this old man, John Jacob, ran a leg of the race. I later learned that he was sixteen years older than me, so twenty-five at the time.

The strange thing about Mr Jacob was that he never came to the annual end of term fancy dress party. I remember my first such party, because halfway through the evening games, a strange Indian man came into the hall begging for "betel nut and paan". He went round everyone begging for "just a few pice". As he went away there was something vaguely familiar about the beggar but I couldn't think why!

*Armenia is a country on the borders of Europe and Asia in an area called the Caucasus or Caucasia, north-east of the Black Sea and close to Turkey and Iran. During the First World War more than a million Armenians were sent to their deaths by the Turkish forces. The details have always been unclear. The Armenians claim they were massacred by the Turkish army when Armenian refugees were left to die of thirst and starvation in the desert. The Turks reject the use of the word massacre since many of their own people died at the same time. Whatever the truth of the event, Christian Armenians and Greeks, were driven out of Turkey and have found new lives in many countries of the world, including the USA and Canada.*

*A large group of Armenians settled in the Bengal part of India, where they developed the jute industry. Jute is a plant with very strong fibres that are used to make sacking and, at one time linoleum in Dundee. My schoolteacher, and later my colleague, John Jacob, grew up in Bengal and found his way to South India.*

The boarding part was a long way from town, or so it seemed, when we walked to and fro. It was called 'Lushington Hall' for reasons which were long forgotten, and we slept in dormitories of locally made wooden beds. Food was a curious mixture of local and British food. I will always remember a green sludge of boiled spinach on toast which appeared once a week for breakfast, allegedly to do us good. My stomach heaves in recollection.

The land around the boarding school was very dramatic. Someone had imported large numbers of eucalyptus trees in the 19th century and they grew vigorously. Their scent was exotic and their leaves a delicate crescent, but their size was enormous. One was felled in the school grounds and measured over 230 feet in height. What was the wood good for? In our case, fuel and rough woodwork. How was it cut up? By two coolies in a sawing pit with a long two handled saw, one man below and another above. India has an abundance of man-power and there will always be coolies looking for manual labour. Hunger hovers over the poor.

The daily walk to school took about twenty minutes in all weathers, which included the monsoon when torrential rain fell over a period of six to eight weeks. We all wore topees, that distinctive colonial headgear, to which we added a water-proof covering when it rained.

On one side of the boarding school there was a steep drop to the gardens which surrounded the residence of the Governor of Madras Province. Many of the wealthy Indians kept hot weather homes and naturally the Governor, the representative of the British Government, had to have something better than the rest. The grounds were technically a Botanic Garden which specialised in local plants. I have memories of playing puddox on a lawn with Cecil Johnson, an encounter that coloured the rest of my life.

Cecil was a staff worker for Scripture Union, a movement whose details appear elsewhere in this book. Every other year he would come to the school for a fortnight of missions. In practice this meant he gave an evangelistic talk on some passage from the Bible, either at morning prayers in the day school or at evening prayers in Lushington. Puddox was a fly to catch a trout or a sprat to catch a whale. It was a crazy mixture of rounders, cricket and rugby. There were two wickets fifteen yards apart like cricket, but instead of running between the wickets you ran at right angles to a single stump. Normal cricket rules applied about stumping and catching etc. The rugby bit was the ball, so large that the least gifted child could hit it enough times to make a game of it.

Cecil would take evening prayers and from it all one thing has stayed with me ever since. He said, "Wouldn't it be very strange if, instead of having three meals a day we saved all the food for one huge meal on a Sunday?" answer: "Yes of course." Yet that is what we do with God's word: we keep it for a Sunday. Wouldn't it be sensible to have a bit every day – some daily bread? And to help us do that, here is a card of Bible readings. Would you like to try it?"

It would be an outrageous lie to say that got me going on Bible reading for the rest of my life: but intermittently it has stuck with me and indeed SU has been a part of my life since then.

Table tennis was the leisure time activity in boarding school. I had never played any kind of game or sport before going to India. Primary school in war time Northern Ireland was a grim business, about reading, writing and 'rithmetic – and a crack across the knuckles with a ruler if you made a mess of it. There were no outdoor games.

My older brother, Ashley, was made to play rugby at grammar school and hated every minute of any kind of sport. In later life, when he had emigrated to Canada, his children forced him to go to at least one baseball game. He took a book, sat in the bleachers and occasionally asked how many rounders had been scored.

Boarding school introduced me to sports, football or cricket in due season. My brother, Ashley, had persuaded me that I couldn't run because my feet were put on wrongly and this was inhibiting. Later in life I discovered that I was actually second eleven/fifteen material and could have been a bit better with a better start. But table tennis showed that I was reasonably well co-ordinated and I had a lot of fun.

Best of all, school introduced me to 'carom' which is spelt in various ways. It is called Indian or poor man's billiards. It is played on a smooth square board with a pocket in each corner. A large white disc is flicked to knock smaller, draughts-sized discs into the pockets and it is all-absorbing. It was a cheap, innocent form of entertainment in a world that never had a radio, let alone TV. Happy days.

## Politics

One major event occurred during the three years I was in India. The first occurred when a friend visited our house one evening with the words "Gandhi is dead." It is difficult now to appreciate the significance of the words. Ghandi, more than anyone else, was the person who enabled India to separate from the British Empire without war or revolution. He was a lawyer who grew up and worked in South Africa. He first came to prominence when the British Government in India introduced a salt tax, which had implications for everyone from the richest to the poorest. He famously adopted the dress of an Indian coolly and went on pilgrimage through India to protest against an iniquitous tax and to promote the idea of independence. At various stages he went on hunger strike to protest against the existence of the British Raj and insisted that India was perfectly capable of governing itself, and that indeed is what happened in 1947.

This is not the place to elaborate on the events that led to the partition of India and Pakistan. It was a time of huge unrest, with massacres by both communities, and turbulent politics. Most of the violence was in the north of India: we in the south were largely unaffected. My one recollection is a debate in school on the motion "Was British rule good for India?" I made a modest contribution to the debate, along the lines of honest law courts free from corruption, and the building of railways. After reading William Dalrymple's books *The Return of a King* and *The Anarchy* I blush with shame for what we actually did, but I also have a quiet satisfaction that there were very commendable aspects of the two centuries when we were in charge.

## *The Anarchy* by William Dalrymple

*Dalrymple's book outlines the opium wars: China wanted silver in exchange for tea, so although the Emperor tried to stop the sale and use of opium in the population, the British grew it in Bengal in large quantities; sold it in China in exchange for silver with which they bought tea. This created huge profits for the East India Company which was then invested in tea-growing in North India e.g at Kalimpong and the Nilgiri Hills round Ooty. This gradually undermined the Chinese monopoly of tea-growing. This trade had to be protected first in the wars won by Clive at the battle of Plessy. As trade grew, India was divided into so many separate Princedoms that there was no real concerted military opposition after Clive. Divide and rule gave*

*Britain astonishing power through a relatively small army which was part Indian. The Mutiny was a rare occurrence.*

When I later asked Indian friends, "What was Britain's most significant contribution to the country?" they usually acknowledged the fairness of the justice system in a country where judicial corruption was a constant threat. The use of the English language across a country which has more than 800 different regional languages was a huge benefit to India, a benefit which continues to this day. The building of a railway network across the whole country was a major unifying factor in a huge country. But it was time for Britain to turn from a colonial past and for India to face a very different future.

## Boarding School in England (1951 – 56)

At that time many children in Britain were familiar with life in Public Schools (meaning a fee-paying, independent school for reasons that are lost in history) because many books – and comics – were set in such schools. 'Comics' also need some explanation. When I returned to Belfast in 1950 my whole week focused on the publication of two boys' comics, the *Wizard* and the *Hotspur*. They had a lot in common because each of them had a war story, a superman story, a football story and a boarding school story. In addition, there were books to read; in my case the all-time favourite were the publications of W.E. Johns featuring Biggles, the wartime and post war hero involved in planes and escaping from impossible, cliff-hanging situations.

The superman heroes were unforgettable. No boy could forget Wilson the first man to climb Everest, swim the Channel, cross the Sahara desert . . . wearing a single garment that looked suspiciously like a pair of old-fashioned combinations, which covered his modesty but left his limbs free to lift boulders above his head; and then his feet were bare, the better to find toe-holds when climbing Everest. What a man! We shall not look upon his like again.

But back to the boarding schools. Billy Bunter sticks in the mind although there were more serious tales. Bunter, the 'Fat Owl of the Remove' – Remove being the name for a particular class rather than anything to do with moving house. Bunter was the only introduction to my next school and the particular ethos of the Public School with Matron, House Masters, cricket and rugger. All this lay ahead.

In September 1951 my parents drove me down to Ramsgate, a coastal town in Kent within sight of the French Coast. It was a red brick building in the shape of an E without the middle stroke. New boys came a day before the rest of the school, giving them an opportunity to settle in. There were 350 pupils, all boys and six 'Houses' into which new boys were placed. The 'Houses' were not separate buildings: the one building contained all boys, but for administrative and competitive reasons the house system was useful and each had its own distinctive character. The Houses made for a competitive environment and inter-house matches on the sports field.

I was introduced to Nick Ranson, another new boy who would be my best friend through and beyond school and we are still in touch. We were each directed to a bed in a dormitory of nine, the first one belonging to a House Prefect who was responsible for discipline – including corporal punishment with a Housemaster's permission. On a shelf above each bed was an ammunition box in which, twice weekly, a ration of socks and handkerchiefs was placed. The windows were wide open to the elements and closed only when rain was actually falling on a bed. In the corridor outside there was a metal wash basin for each boy. Wartime conditions still applied, in that sweets were rationed, and much of the equipment, such as the ammunition boxes, were relics of the army.

Looking back I can see that the whole system had several fundamental aims: first, to occupy every minute of the day to minimise trouble: second, to devolve responsibility for discipline to dependable older boys, including judicious powers of punishment, thus saving staff time and money, so there were house prefects and school prefects. Overall power lay with the Head and the staff, but in practice they were little in evidence. The payoff to the boys came in the form of minor honours: small privileges, like staying up late, having or sharing a study and wearing blazers with ribbons for sporting success. This time-honoured system worked well and was cheap.

The daily routine fulfilled the central purpose of keeping everyone occupied. A bell rang at 6.30 am and there was a roll call every morning at 7.30, by which time everyone was to be in the house common room. Defaulters had two warnings and then the cane: two strokes on the backside administered by the Housemaster, although this could be delegated to a prefect in some circumstances. It is interesting that this was accepted without question at the time, and had been since time immemorial: *autre moeurs, autre temps.*

(Read *Tom Brown's School Days* and you will see that our situation was a vast improvement over our grandfathers' time. Lord Shaftesbury, the great 19th century social reformer, said his school days at Harrow were "nasty, degrading and wicked". I suspect the aim was to make life so unpleasant that military service on land or sea could only be an improvement.)

I won't enlarge on the five years at school. In due course I passed exams, played sport at second fifteen level in rugby, hockey and cricket, and swam breaststroke for the school. There was a Cadet Force for Army, Navy and Air force. I played the tenor drum in the band. All this worked out very well for me. Remember, National Service hovered ominously over school leavers. Healthy males of eighteen were required to serve two years in one of the Forces. I had chosen to be in the RAF section of the Corps and there were several benefits. One summer holiday I did a gliding course at Cambridge airfield and got my solo certificates A and B. I just wish I could have afforded this very expensive hobby in later life. The joy of flying solo in a plane that makes no noise, but the sound of the wind, is beyond description. Indeed, on one occasion flying in an open cockpit with the instructor, we got into a wonderful thermal that took us up above two thousand feet and we looped the loop with everyone watching below. The instructor knew there would be a row when we landed, but it was too late – and worth the penalty.

The second great benefit was that I could be pre-selected for Air Crew while still at school. The result was that without delay I could get my call-up papers and go straight to RAF for officer and flying training.

One obvious question arises: where did the money come from for my expensive education? When I went to Boarding School in 1951 I got a scholarship for £80 towards annual fees of £350. The gap was covered by a grant from Middlesex County Council and that continued through to University. I will always be grateful to the Labour Government for this policy of providing education for all – even those who probably voted Tory.

When I graduated, I wrote MCC a letter of profuse thanks but never got a reply. I guess they didn't have a department dealing with gratitude.

Pocket money came from the occasional pound or two from friends or relatives and was greatly appreciated. Once I joined the RAF it seemed I had wealth beyond the dreams of avarice, because it was on top of all living costs.

## National Service (1956 – 58)

I was the last of the National Servicemen. After the second world war, the government decided that in addition to a standing army, there was also a need to have trained civilians in case of war, and that was National Service, which lasted two years and could be in any of the three services. What was it like? It could be very boring or it could be very exciting.

However, I joined the RAF at a critical point in British history when there was a real threat of war involving Britain, France, Egypt and the 'super-powers', America and Russia. Britain and France had built the Suez Canal in 1869 but in 1956 the Egyptian Government, led by Colonel Nasser, nationalised the canal, thus depriving Britain and France of income and ownership of the canal. Britain and France invaded Egypt to regain control and there was a real threat that Russia might support Egypt in a war which would involve Britain and the USA. The new Great Powers – Russia and the USA – demanded a withdrawal and thence the resignation of Anthony Eden the British Prime Minister. It was the most humiliating incident in British post-war history.

My older brother, who happened to be visiting from Canada, shook my hand as he left and said, "This is the beginning of World War three: I don't think we will meet again." I think I detected a hope that at last he might be freed from his pesty younger brother. So what was national service like?

Officer training was pretty tedious but began when I arrived, with a dozen or so other trainees, at Kirton-in-Lindsay railway station in Lincolnshire. We were met by an Irish RAF Sergeant whose first words were, "You will refer to me on all occasions as 'Sir': I will also address you trainees as 'Sir'. The difference is that you will mean it." It was a neat summary of our respective positions. We learned how to write formal letters to superior officers; in which direction to pass the port at formal dinners; we bashed a lot of squares; we did route marches across ploughed fields in bulled (highly polished) boots and we wrote daily diaries about the Suez Crisis which was unfolding at the time: we passed out as the lowest form of officer life, Acting Pilot Officers, until  we completed the course and gained our wings, after which we were Pilot Officers.

Think of me, if you can, in January 1957, sailing First Class as an RAF officer, in a Cunard ship across the Atlantic to Halifax, Nova Scotia, Canada. For the first and only time in my life, I ate an eight-course dinner. Behind me were three months of officer training and I was en route to Winnipeg for a year's flying training to be a navigator. I shall never forget the magical train journey in the depth of winter, through a pristine, snowbound wilderness of trees and frozen lakes. I was entranced at hour after unbroken hour through this endless Christmas card. Even better was the journey round the north shore of Lake Superior, sitting in the observation dome in the moonlight. I was welcomed in Winnipeg with a temperature of –40 centigrade. With a new uniform went the giddy pleasure of a salary, freedom, buying a car, meeting actual girls after five years in a boys only boarding school.

## Navigation

*How did planes navigate with only the basic instruments used in the second world war?*

*Our planes were equipped with a radio direction compass. This could be tuned into any radio source and it would give a bearing on the source, relative to plane's direction, e.g. "Radio Winnipeg, bearing 194 degrees [meaning it was behind the plane] and 14 degrees on the port side." If you then got a visual compass bearing on a passing grain elevator of 90 degrees on the starboard side you could plot that on your chart and your position would then be where the two bearings intersected, but of course you also had to take an exact time check and move the first line forward to intersect with the second position line.*

*The same procedure could be done at night, taking bearings on stars or planets, using a sextant in a plastic dome on top of the cabin. This required a lot of time and patience.*

*The most memorable event in my training takes a little explanation. One of the more advanced exercises involved flying without a compass and using a gyroscope instead. A rapidly spinning gyro maintains its position – much as the turning of a cycle wheel keeps the bike upright – except that nothing is perfect. Although the planes we flew in had good gyros, they still precessed, or drifted slowly from their initial direction. But the problem was how much did the gyro precess and how could we correct it? The answer was that while I navigated the plane, the Assistant Navigator measured the precession by taking a position line on the sun. If the gyro precessed, let us say, five degrees to starboard of our direction, he would correct the gyro by moving it ten degrees in the opposite direction. Sadly, he did not apply the ten degrees in the opposite direction but added it in the same direction, so every fifteen minutes we would be turning fifteen degrees away from where should have been going. Do this for long enough and you go round in a circle.*

*The result was that our pilot came on the intercom to say, "In five minutes, we will be entering the airspace of the USA for which you have no permission. Unless you do something very quickly two fighter jets will intercept us to see if we are Russian aircraft coming to do harm. Please give me a new heading at your earliest convenience."*

*Pilots are courteous lads (a better class of bus driver, really), but with a weakness for irony. Of course, technically all this was my fault because as first navigator I had responsibility to check the second navigator's calculations, but instead I was looking at a wilderness of lakes and forest in western Ontario trying to find a landmark, but because of the giro error we were far from where I was looking.*

We had a second tense moment some months later. There were enough Brits in training to make up a cricket team and the RCAF generously offered to take us to any other cricket team we could locate. Winnipeg is more or less in the middle of Canada and the team we located was in Victoria, British Columbia, about 1,500 miles away. A promise is a promise, so in one of our usual Dakota planes we flew over the Rockies, and down the Fraser valley, across Vancouver and out to Victoria on Vancouver Island. The setting for the cricket match was quintessentially English with elderly gents in deck chairs saying "Jolly good shot sir!" Victoria was much loved by British emigrants who retired from the fierce winter temperatures in east and central Canada to the milder climates of the pacific coast.

However, there was a critical moment as we were flying in cloud over the Rockies and our starboard engine suddenly stopped, giving us a maximum altitude of 10,000 feet when the highest peaks were higher than that. I remember locating the nearest parachute but then realised that it would not be much use when we did hit something solid.

## Survival Exercises

One experience in our training turned out to be more useful than I knew at the time. Since we would be flying over many uninhabited parts of Canada in all weathers, including possible spells at −40 centigrade, it was important for us to have some survival skills. Accordingly, we went off with instructors to a remote forest in February with the exact equipment which would always fly with us, including an axe, a shotgun, army survival rations of a particularly tasteless recipe; a sleeping bag, a knife for each of us, a whistle for emergency communication and – a box of matches. We had been told how to build a lean-to shelter with a wall of timber logs in front of it to reflect into the sleeping/living space the heat of a fire which was to burn throughout our stay. Then appropriate leaves and branches were cut down to make bedding that would keep us off the ground through the night. It was also, of course, an exercise in teamwork. We were warned about the dangers of getting lost in a forest which probably covered about a thousand square miles and in which we might never be located.

In fairness the temperature was only –25 C but the big question on the first morning was, "Who let the fire go out?"

As regards food, we had one additional element to add to the survival rations. I went with another guy to find something edible to shoot and sure enough we hadn't gone far when we saw a spruce hen sitting on a branch maybe twenty feet away. She looked at us with the puzzled expression of a botanist viewing a new species.

"Well, go on: shoot it."

"It's like shooting my Granny at close range."

"It's food, stupid. Shoot it."

"You shoot it. It's not your Granny."

Bang! An explosion of feathers and about 5 ounces of meat under the plucked feathers. We boiled it but the survival rations weren't at all bad.

It was all good training for the event that never happened and possibly we were a little better trained for family picnics.

## Night Flying up North

While we were training, major innovations in navigation were coming to fruition. The Doppler effect, namely the thing you hear when an ambulance blowing its horn rises in pitch as it comes towards you and then drops as it goes away, was used for the first time to navigate a plane across the Atlantic. A plane emitting two high frequency tones forward and two back found its way very accurately from Europe to America. Its main problem was that enemy scanners could pick up the transmissions too easily. Other land-based aids were also coming on stream, so the skills of using a sextant inside a plastic dome on the top of an elderly Dakota might never be needed – except in an emergency. To the best of my knowledge at one time all planes included a very sophisticated version of the sextant in case all its navigational aids defaulted. As far as I know, that is still the case.

*One reason why the Canadian Air force trained their pilots to use non-electronic aids was that the magnetic north pole is located in northwest Canada and several hundred miles from the geographical pole. One nice result of this is that we got wonderful aurora effects quite frequently, but the pole plays havoc with magnetic compasses as you approach magnetic north. I therefore learned how to take a two-minute sextant shot on a star, by looking through an eye piece and holding the star in the middle of a tiny bubble. Three of these two-minute sights produce three position lines which ideally would produce a single crossing point – provided you made allowance for the fact the plane had been in constant motion during that time.*

*It was a dying skill – but I am proud that I may have been one of a small group of people who have actually done it.*

## Family Interlude

By a happy chance I was able to be best man at my brother Ashley's wedding. He had emigrated to Montreal and his engagement was announced shortly before I arrived to do National Service and I was able not only to get leave to be his best man, but the RCAF flew me from Winnipeg to Montreal in time – just – to do the job. It was a memorable flight because we hit a thunderstorm over Ontario and I have a vivid memory of watching the altimeter drop over a thousand feet in a few seconds.

It was a unique wedding in that there were three sets of identical twins: Ashley's wife was one, my sister Joyce was one and my mother also was one and all three sets were together for the celebrations. I had a month's holiday halfway through the course and was able to spend it with my family in Montreal. It was the last time we were all able to be together.

And then a dramatic development. Towards the end of our year of flying, all British trainees were gathered on parade for a formal announcement: "Due to a change in government policy, National Service will be ended as soon as trainees have completed their course."

We completed the course and were awarded our Navigators' wings on a Friday and on Monday we were civilians. I chose to stay in Canada for the next six months to be with a married brother and a married sister who lived in Montreal. For six months I worked in a tea-tasters' office, making countless cups of tea for the 'Tasters' who were men with years of experience. Every few weeks we would receive hundreds of chests of teas from the tea growing parts of the world, including the Nilgiri hills mentioned above where I had my early schooling. These teas were bought and sold at auctions, mainly in London and each batch from an estate would have very distinct qualities which were discernible – after about six years of experience gained by standing next to an experienced man. My job, after dealing with bills of lading and getting everything through customs, was to set out a dozen cups (without handles) with information about the origin of the tea. Each bowl would be given a description as the tasters slurped it loudly (all part of the craft). This description later enabled the chests of tea, from various sources, to be blended together to maintain constant standards for the benefit of the paying public.

When I gave in my resignation, explaining that I had a place to study at Oxford, they said, "You'll make more money as a tea taster," and they were probably right.

# Chapter 2 Oxford (1956 – 59)

My grandchildren are now going to university and I marvel at the accommodation available – with pity. Modern students seem to live in a large cupboard, with just enough space to fit in a bed, a desk and a tiny shower room. When I tell them that in my first year in college I had, for my own personal use, a large ground-floor sitting room or study, probably a bit larger than a suburban drawing room, with a bedroom attached. My room was cleaned and my tea dishes washed by a college 'scout' who was an ex-army man. I shared a bathroom on the landing with the person on the other ground floor room. In the second and third years I shared suburban lodgings, or digs, with my friend, Harvey Glasgow.

Endless books and memoirs have been written about university life but a few things stick out in my memory. The first was the tutorial system which is potentially frightening but was actually a huge privilege and pleasure. Studying English Language and Literature, I had one hour per week face to face with the Reverend Ralph Houghton to read him an essay and discuss it. Ralph was a classicist originally, who took responsibility for English students. He was nearing retirement and was a window into a gentler, Victorian age. While I was in Canada, I received a reading list that I was encouraged to get through in advance of coming up. My Canadian brother-in-law assured me that I was the only person in the whole of Montreal who went to work on the back of a colleague's Lambretta scooter – carrying the complete works of Shakespeare for light reading in lunch break. He was probably right.

Anglo-Saxon was taught at St Edmund's Hall by an engaging Australian whose name escapes me, but he was well-known for his DPhil thesis on 'subordinate clauses in Anglo-Saxon poetry' in which he examined all extant texts in excruciating detail. However, he evoked in many of us a love for the ancient poem 'The Seafarer' in which the poet described, all the miseries of sailing across the oceans in, what we would call, a Viking boat, and therefore open to all the elements. But then there is a change when he says, in effect, that nonetheless when he hears the cry of the seagulls something in him stirs and he longs, in spite of everything, to go to sea again.

The time for journeys would come and my soul
Called me eagerly out, sent me over
The horizon, seeking foreigners' homes.
But there isn't a man on earth so proud,
So born to greatness, so bold with his youth,
Grown so grave, or so graced by God,
That he feels no fear as the sails unfurl,
Wondering what fate has willed and will do.

When I was doing my teacher training in Aberdeen one of the tutors was a former BBC producer who gave us the task of making a radio programme about a subject of our choice. It happened that I had once – and only once – gone to sea for a week on an Aberdeen fishing trawler, skippered by a lovely old friend, Johnny Mair. My main memory was seasickness every hour on the hour but I remembered Johnny saying that although he could drink all he loved of the sea and "it would do me no harm," yet when I retired and heard the foghorns going at the harbour entrance, despite everything, "something in me longed once again to be going to sea" – just like 'The Seafarer'. I made a wee radio programme about it.

Another hour per week, was with Robert Burchfield who was the Editor of the Oxford English Dictionary. I had never given any thought to how dictionaries are compiled, and I am so glad that I worked on the project during a vacation. The O.E.D. was begun in the 1930s and will continue into the indefinite future because new words and meanings will always emerge. Burchfield's job was to collect words and their usage from current books and publications and to this end he had about a hundred volunteers from many walks of life who regularly sent in letters illustrating the use and the source of new words. For example, a few years ago the most widely used new word was 'selfie' which reflected technological change.

Robert's task was to bring the dictionary up to date with words introduced between 1930 (when the previous edition had stopped) up to 1970, I think. It was a task which demanded, and in his case received, meticulous care and thought. I bumped into him twenty-two years after he had started and he had by then just published the third of four volumes. The work continues but I think he died before his task was quite finished.

Of course, with modern technology this task has become much simpler than what the earlier editors had to cope with.

I remember his gentle chastisement when I was ten minutes late for a tutorial. "I don't much care for lateness." I didn't do it again.

J.R.R. Tolkein 'lectured' regularly in the main lecture hall but every week he was 'indisposed', allegedly adding more material to the *Lord of the Rings*. (This cannot be confirmed but was widely suspected.) His son, Christopher, gave me an hour lecture on 'Sound Changes in Old Norse' but that was enough for a lifetime on that particular subject.

The first hurdle to be negotiated was Prelims at the end of the second term of the first year and the object was to see that candidates were working, or whether they had been admitted without sufficient scrutiny. There was a paper on Anglo-Saxon literature which was mainly *Beowulf* for translation and analysis, and a paper on either Greek or Latin epic poetry, Homer or Virgil. There were two books of the Aeneid which I think I learnt by heart.

These Greek and Latin epic poems were the basis for Milton's *Paradise Lost* which was the special interest of Dame Helen Gardner and I can hear her declaiming the opening lines in a deep, solemn tone:

Of man's first disobedience and the fruit of that forbidden tree
whose mortal taste brought death into the world and all our woe . . .

It was while Studying Milton and *Paradise Lost* that something struck me for the first time. Subject choices at school are often made on our attitude, positive or negative, to the teachers involved. I was never blessed with an inspiring history teacher and chose to do sciences instead. It was while reading Paradise Lost that I discovered that Milton had been the private secretary to Oliver Cromwell, leader of the Parliamentary forces against the King in the English Civil War 1642–51. Suddenly poetry had a context! Why would Milton want to "justify the ways of God to man", which, he said, was his purpose in writing the poem?

*Paradise Lost* tells the Biblical story of Adam and Eve, their expulsion from the Garden of Eden, 'the fall of man' to use the theological term. On the face of it, the whole of the magnificent poem is a theological statement about why the world and humanity, are in the parlous state we now live in "with all our woe," living under the righteous judgment of God against human sin. But if human sin occurs because of Satan's temptation of Eve, and if Satan is a fallen angel cast out of heaven for rebellion, then surely the ultimate reason for 'the Fall' is God's punishment of Satan and therefore God, and the freedom he gives to his creatures, is the source of evil? This conundrum is the basis for Milton's very long poem of 'justification' for Adam and Eve's punishment which followed, as we read it in the Bible. It is a very long argument and not many readers follow the argument to its conclusion.

But perhaps there was an additional context for the poem. His commanding officer, Cromwell, would eventually have King Charles the First, God's anointed, executed. How could this be justified? Was Milton involved in two parallel attempts to relate theology to the world of war and politics: the Biblical story and the English civil war? Was Oliver Cromwell, Milton's boss, also trying to justify rebellion against his King and the oath he had sworn to serve him? Did Milton and Cromwell have long theological and political discussions about the theology of regicide? Did Cromwell die with a clear conscience? Did Milton?

All was well, which meant no more exams until finals at the end of the third year.

I had a few close friends and a lot of acquaintances. Harvey Glasgow captained our college hockey team, in which I played – without any particular distinction. I tried to persuade Harvey to take up rowing for what I think were called 'summer eights' and were designed for people who wanted the experience of rowing without taking it seriously. (He chickened out.) The competition usually involved six (?) boats of the kind familiar to anyone who has watched the Boat Race against Cambridge, with the difference that six boats start out one behind the other at a distance of one and a half boat lengths between each. Thus, when the starting gun goes, your boat chases and tries to 'bump' the boat in front by gently (?) swinging your bow against its stern. At different times in life I have been physically tired, really tired, but I have never longed so much to stop as in these Bumps races, partly because you are not just trying to bump the guy in front but the one behind wants to bump you. Never again.

Harvey had many of the virtues I lacked, such as thorough preparation for life. He did Philosophy, Politics and Economics and then went on to qualify as an accountant. We are still good friends.

David Alexander was a good friend until his early death. He and his wife Pat set up their own Lion Publishing company and produced a wide range of (very readable) Christian books including their first major project, *The Lion Handbook to the Bible*, which quickly sold more than a million copies, then *The Lion History of Christianity* and many more. These were ground-breaking in their use of illustration and innovative design and layout. Very sadly, David was one of the first people to catch lyme disease which was first identified in the USA as a disease caried by ticks on deer, but deadly for human beings. David would have died of it, despite the attentions of excellent doctors in the Radcliffe Infirmary in Oxford. His life was saved by a young American doctor who had knowledge of this new disease. However, David's health was permanently damaged, and he died some years later.

## Oxford Vacations (1957 – 59)

When I left Montreal and the tea business my dear sister Joyce, with whom I had lodged for six months, gave back to me all the rent I had paid her for my lodging. It was typical of her. At the end of my first year, I used the money to buy a Lambretta (scooter). It was unfashionable in that it had a windscreen: derisive laughter from the bright young things, but I was going to use it for long journeys: not for hanging about coffee bars with mods and rockers. I drove to Aberdeen and from there back to Oxford and in the summer vacation I went to the continent. There was a good college friend, the only son of a farmer, who had never been abroad, so I encouraged him to buy a scooter and we crossed to the continent: his first experience of abroad. Every day was a character-building experience for both of us. Ken's idea of a good day's travel was somewhere between 30 and 60 miles: I had a whole continent to cover before my money ran out.

We stayed in 'Jugend Herberge': German Youth Hostels, and they were excellent. Germany was still recovering from the second world war but they had made much better progress than we Brits in their orderliness and organisation. What was pretty hard to take was that young Germans in the youth hostels had a bad habit of singing lusty rustic songs at us – and then demanding that we sing some of our folk songs. Eh . . .? Our German went very little beyond "Wo is der Haupt Bahnhoff, bitte?" Once in the railway station most things could be found from there.

By mutually agreed stages we travelled up the Rhine, living on little beyond bread and cheese, with the occasional squandering on raspberry tart and cream: food for the gods. By and large the weather was kind to us through the Black Forest to Donaueschingen where the river Danube starts and then flows past four capital cities: Vienna, Bratislava, Budapest and Belgrade. These were fascinating names that suggested a whole continent to be explored in due course, which eventually happened after I married Hilda.

We made it into Switzerland as far as Zermatt and other tourist spots, and then headed for Ken's home where his Mum produced a lordly plate of bacon, eggs and mushrooms that was rare to see. Foreign food is OK but there is nothing like mother's best.

From there it was home to Aberdeen. On other occasions, such as the end of a term, I could drive to Aberdeen by picking up a delivery car for my brother-in-law's Ford dealership. In the 1950s, the car had to be picked up from the Ford factory in Dagenham and then 'run in'. This will be a strange word to people under the age of sixty or thereabouts. What it meant was that the machining of engine parts was not an exact science, so the engine should be driven at no more than fifty m.p.h. for the first five hundred miles, giving time for any rough edges to be slowly worn away.

This meant driving all the way to Aberdeen being overtaken and hooted at by vehicles on roads built long before the first motorways. Indeed, during that time Britain was only just by-passing, with dual carriageways, major town bottlenecks like Grantham and Newark. So a day's drive would get me just over the Scottish border to a Youth Hostel where nobody demanded that you sing your favourite folk song. There were a good many honest Scottish songs sung but they were entirely voluntary. After breakfast next morning I could be in Aberdeen by noon. Happy days.

## India

My second summer vacation was very memorable because my lovely family clubbed together and bought me a return air fare to see my parents, who were working in Madras, South India. There was icing on the cake in that I flew out in one of the very early Boeing 707s. With the Comet, Britain had won the race to put the first passenger jet plane into service; the Americans, with their greater resources, were later but took the main prize in size and number.

Madras is down at the coast of south-east India and is therefore hot and humid. I found this initially so tiring that the family wanted their money back since I was sleeping long hours at night and at siesta. My parents timed their annual holiday in the cool air of Ooty until I came out, so we drove the three hundred or so miles back to my birthplace and all the old memories flooded back: the smells of eucalyptus, and *vadai* – a large, thin pancake full of potato curry, from the cafes; the cries of *jatheeka, jatheeka, jatheeka warleblong* from the street sellers; I never did find out what they were selling but the words stick in my mind. There was the old school – and the attached memories. There were the Botanic Gardens, now open always to the public since there was no British Provincial Governor, and Lushington Hall. The old school building in town had been sold and the entire school was now at Lushington, with pupils coming from many Asian countries by plane and train. I asked, and they still had a fancy dress party at the end of the term, but Mr Jacob had gone on to other things. They said they never got green spinach on toast for breakfast: slime had been abolished despite the health-giving benefits claimed for it.

For much of my young life I had an irrational desire to go to Nepal and the Himalayas and in the goodness of my family and the residual savings from the RAF, I took the train from Madras to Calcutta. (The city's name takes a number of forms. At the time of writing it is Kolkata, I think.) My main memory was of a businessman who shared the compartment. He spent a lot of time denouncing the endemic corruption in Indian business and politics.

"There are only two honest men in India: the Prime Minister . . ."

"And yourself?" I suggested.

He looked at me in astonishment: "Are you crazy?" he asked. "You can't survive in India if you are honest." I never did discover who the second honest man was. He was making a serious point, and maybe what he says applies the world over. Can a truly honest businessman make a living in India – or Britain?

I had no particular destination in Calcutta beyond a bit of sight-seeing and then a train up the Ganges to Patna and a flight into Nepal, but as I got off a bus in the city centre I saw, of all unexpected things, a building with the words 'William Carey Baptist Church' and that is the name of a very great man. (Churchill had a habit of reminding his wife that he was 'a very great man' when she was inclined to nag, but Carey's greatness was of a very different kind.

Here is the Wikipedia extract:

*William Carey (17 August 1761 – 9 June 1834) was an English Christian missionary, Particular Baptist minister, translator, social reformer and cultural anthropologist who founded the Serampore College and the Serampore University, the first degree-awarding university in India.*

*He went to Calcutta (Kolkata) in 1793, but was forced to leave the British Indian territory by Anglican and non-Baptist Christian missionaries. He joined the Baptist missionaries in the Danish colony of Frederiksnagar in Serampore. One of his first contributions was to start schools for impoverished children where they were taught reading, writing, accounting and Christianity. He opened the first theological university in Serampore offering divinity degrees, and campaigned to end the practice of sati, meaning the custom of a widow being burnt on the funeral pyre of her husband,*

*Carey is known as 'the father of modern missions'. His essay, 'An Enquiry into the Obligations of Christians to Use Means for the Conversion of the Heathens', led to the founding of the Baptist Missionary Society. The Asiatic Society commended Carey for "his eminent services in opening the stores of Indian literature to the knowledge of Europe and for his extensive acquaintance with the science, the natural history and botany of this country and his useful contributions, in every branch."*

*He translated the Hindu classic, the Ramayana, into English, and the Bible into Bengali, Oriya, Assamese, Marathi, Hindi and Sanskrit.*

*William Carey has been called a reformer and an illustrious Christian missionary.*

By any standards these are extraordinary achievements, but he was a cobbler by trade: he taught himself at least four languages to enable him to understand the Bible better, but also to make it more easily understood. The title of his work, *An Enquiry into the Obligations of Christians to Use Means for the Conversion of the Heathens*, sounds strange to modern ears. What it meant was that God would not magically bring people of other races to faith in God through Jesus Christ: he would use other means to accomplish that goal, namely individual people using all their gifts and enduring all kinds of opposition to accomplish that end. In his case it included losing his wife to the extreme conditions in which they lived in India.

The opposition to his work from other missionaries, mainly Anglican, was understandable at the time. During the Reformation, theology was integrated in the politics of each country and deviation from the state's religion was considered rebellion, so Carey was a non-conformist: in theory at least, a traitor to his native country and therefore expelled from the British settlement in Calcutta. His great Baptist predecessor, John Bunyan suffered imprisonment for the same fault, but happily wrote *Pilgrim's Progress* while in jail.

Carey had to begin his ministry on an island cut off from his English compatriots. His achievements speak for themselves, not only in church matters but in his service to India, as outlined above. His openness to Indian languages and culture, as listed above is extraordinary, as well as the teaching of poor children. His opposition and campaigning against 'sati', the custom where a Hindu widow would cast herself on the funeral pyre of her dead husband, would have made many enemies, but it was an issue throughout the years of British presence in India.

Carey is remembered for many things which could be summed up in his favourite epigram:

"Expect great things from God; attempt great things for God."

My main memory of Calcutta was the buses. There is an official maximum to the number of passengers a bus may take, but in practice there is no maximum, including those standing on the bumpers at the back and front. I have never been jammed up against so many bodies. Breathing was possible, but only just.

## Nepal

Many of us have the memory of a single book that transformed our ideas, or directed our lives, or created a hunger for some experience. As a boy growing up in south India, my whole understanding of North India was coloured by Jim Corbett's book, *Man-eaters of Kumaon*. Jim was no ordinary army officer trying to bag a tiger skin for his study floor back at home. Jim was a woodsman with a profound love and knowledge of the jungles and wildlife of the Himalayan foothills. His books came from the many times when he was called out to a village where a woman, cutting grass for her cow, was grabbed by a tiger which, for some reason, had been injured and was no longer able to catch a deer or other wild animal and had turned to human kills for its food. Jim 's profound understanding of wildlife enabled him to track a tiger to its kill and often identify the injury that had made it a menace to local farmers. As a boy I had read most of his books and in later life I have re-read them with nostalgic delight.

But beyond the Indian foothills of the Himalayas, which were the country covered by Rudyard Kipling, lay Nepal and Mount Everest. Nepal was the country from which the British and Indian governments had for more than a century recruited Gurkha soldiers who were legendary for their fortitude, bravery and military skills.

There are endless stories about the bravery and resourcefulness of Ghurkhas. My favourite was about the soldier who was wounded in the Malayan insurgency and got separated from his unit. He found his way back to Nepal with the help of a map which he had found – of the London Underground!

Above all, Everest, Kangchenjunga and the highest peaks were all in Nepal and I wanted, at the very least, to set foot in the country. It was only a few years before my visit that Nepal had finally opened to the world beyond its boundaries. The various rulers of Nepal had very jealously guarded their freedom from inclusion in British India.

That did not necessarily prevent intrepid people from sneaking in illegally, including one of my Antarctic friends, but it was only after the conquest of Everest in 1953 that Nepal opened its doors to tourists.

My route to Nepal took me up the Ganges River by train to Patna, where an elderly Dakota reminded me of my flying days, but there was no navigator required. When the passengers were on board, a magnificent Sikh with the inevitable turban was the last to enter. He went into the cockpit, started the engines, took off in a spiral climb and headed north for 145 miles to *Kathmandu*. I am quite glad I didn't have a window seat because the single runway at that time was carved out of a steep slope which ended in a precipitous drop after a worryingly short runway but the Sikh pilot carried it off with casual ease – and ten yards or so to spare.

I found a hotel for the night and the décor and furnishings must have been unchanged for a century or more. It was magical: a four-poster bed complete with perfumed curtains. Next morning, I walked the streets of Kathmandu. The great joy of wandering was that I seemed to be the only European. There were few signs of western influence: just a long succession of Buddhist temples and the all-pervading scent of incense burning. The surrounding hills obscured the sight of the great mountain peaks, but there was time for that later. I had arranged to meet staff at a Christian hospital that for some years had been serving the city population and it was there that I later met Dr Lily O'Hanlon, a name widely known and respected in north India. For many years she had hoped to get residence in Nepal but the Nepalese policy remained firm, so she established a dispensary in India, close to the Nepalese border and offered medical treatment to all who could access it.

At a Christian hospital in Kathmandu, which had been built to provide services to the country, I met Dr O'Hanlan, as I had hoped. A broken arm had brought her into the new Mission hospital in Kathmandu and I heard her story. Long before Nepal was opened to foreigners following the conquest of Everest, Dr O'Hanlon and a woman colleague felt the need to set up a small dispensary to serve people on the main trade route from India into Nepal, and for a good many years they healed wounds, set broken limbs, prescribed pills and did the best they could for all who needed it.

The happy accident, for me at least, of her broken arm gave me the chance to hear an account of many of the trials and privations she had faced in setting up a working hospital at a place called Pokrah. The cover of her book, *A Mission Hospital at the foot of Fish-Tail Mountain in* Nepal, reminds me of her great contribution to Nepal.

AT THE FOOT
OF THE
FISH-TAIL MOUNTAIN
by LILY M. O'HANLON

This little book is considered by the staff of the International Nepal Fellowship to be the most significant publication in the mission's history. Following the opening of Nepal's borders to ex-patriate missionaries in 1952, it tells of the story of founding of the mission work at the Shining Hospital in Pokhara. (Rob, 21 May 2018)

Lily O'Hanlon was one of many single women who had a call to remote parts of the world. Between the two world wars there were three remarkable women called Mildred Cable, Eva and Francesca French, who travelled to remote parts of Central Asia where they not only spread the Gospel but also made detailed reports to British cartographers of places that had never been explored by Europeans. In their book *Across the Ghobi Desert*, (which they crossed three times) they took and distributed literature in many languages.

Gladys Aylward's work in China was made into a film called *The Inn of the Sixth Happiness*. Mary Slessor, a mill worker from Dundee went to Nigeria and was greatly influential in the area she worked, and there were many more. Dr O'Hanlon's work complemented theirs by working in a small area, but one where many thousands of people passed her door.

I would have loved more than anything to have gone some way up the Everest trail but time, money and politics made it impossible. The best I could do was a stiff walk out of the city and up into the hills for a distant glimpse and a photograph of the high snow peaks. Later, in the plane I had a good sight of Annapurna. Since then, I have been an avid reader of books of exploration and travel.

Then a most extraordinary coincidence occurred. I went into a small hotel to get a bite of lunch and at the next table were two British men whom I instantly recognised. Both had trained as pilots in Canada, while I did my Navigator course and, presumably, they were in Nepal for some particular reason. Their story was that they had really caught the flying bug and wanted to do something positive for humanity – and fly – if they could find some worthwhile humanitarian project which justified the expense – which would have to be raised somehow.

While much of the world was pre-occupied by the second world war, the Chinese army had invaded and occupied Tibet, the roof of the world. The fiercest opposition to the Chinese came from tribespeople called Cambas. They were nomads who had fled to Nepal and India where they were an embarrassment to the respective governments. My friends had espoused their cause and had raised money to fly out to Nepal in order to interview them and present their case to the world at large.

Much of our conversation focused on how they raised the money from a sceptical public; how they could afford to hire a small plane, a Piper Cub, if I remember rightly, and how did they manage to find their way from Britain to Nepal without the aid of an experienced navigator – like me? I don't remember that any great change happened to the unfortunate Camba tribespeople as the result of their advocacy, but they had an exciting time.

The money had been raised by latching on to the public indignation against the invading Chinese and their hostility to the Cambas. They were two good-looking, articulate guys who had sympathetic journalistic contacts. As for the plane they were able to get a friendly lease by mentioning the persecuted Cambas, and they had navigated their way across Europe and the Middle East in twelve shortish journeys between British military bases and commercial airports, but it was a grim struggle against sand storms and shortages of petrol. I offered the interesting fact that I had flown out in one of the earliest Boeing 707s. The amount they were offering for my ticket was so high I almost sold it.

Then it was the Sikh and the Dakota to fly down to Agra and Delhi and a Boeing 707 to home.

## The Last Year at Oxford

In my last year, I moved with Harvey to new digs a little further from town. My landlady had fairly recently taken in lodgers, having given up a good job with a publisher because, in her own words, he was a crook. His name was Robert Maxwell.

There are many descriptions of final examinations. The English department had a long-standing tradition that everything you had absorbed, as opposed to merely crammed at the final hour, was best tested by nine three-hour papers between Friday morning and the following Tuesday afternoon. The papers came in chronological order with Anglo-Saxon first on Thursday morning and then on to the ninth paper on Tuesday afternoon. This was a more or less open invitation to write about any author who had made a particular impression on you.

My college tutor had a quaint tradition of inviting his five students for a picnic beside the river Windrush in the Cotswolds, that quintessentially English area of old villages and charming countryside. His argument was that the exams were a test of what you had absorbed in three years rather than crammed in the last three months (or weeks) so there was nothing to be gained by burning midnight oil. He was probably right and I would not have discovered the Windrush without it.

All five of us got second class honours.

# Chapter 3  Antarctica (1961 – 64)

Then what? For two years I had shared digs with my good friend Harvey Glasgow: We were very different. He had done PPE (Philosophy, Politics and Economics) and later went on to qualify as a chartered accountant, like his father. Through our final year Harvey carefully gathered lots of information about potential jobs, weighing up their various merits, including pensions, whereas I could think of nothing I really wanted to do. Another close friend, David Alexander, went into publishing but that horrified me. I had been interviewed for a couple of jobs with computer companies and had been offered a job. I turned it down. I wanted to travel.

## The Next Step

I spent about ten hours a day in the library leading up to Finals, with a break to read the job adverts in the paper. One day the word ANTARCTICA in bold letters leapt off the page and then the words "Meteorologists required" and I immediately sent off an application with no prospect of success. But then, against all expectations, I was asked to attend an interview with the Falkland Islands Dependencies Survey (FIDS for short) at the Commonwealth Office in London.

I now believe I got the job under false pretences. I gave, as one of my referees, George Barton, the Headmaster of Robert Gordon's College in Aberdeen, who was a great friend of brother-in-law Stephen. As a referee, he was asked a series of questions about my suitability for polar life and was then required to award a mark between 0 and 5 where five was best. Many of the questions were about my likely behaviour in stressful conditions, personality conflicts, loneliness, isolation, months of darkness, and so on. Needless to say, George couldn't answer them, so he asked Stephen's opinion. Allegedly, Stephen said, "Let's get rid of him: give him five for everything," so I got the job.

Here is a piece of gratuitous advice: if you plan to write a very modest book about travelling, never read at the same time Sir Ranulph Fiennes' book, *Mad, Bad and Dangerous to Know*. I have not walked across Antarctica or circum-navigated the world via the north and south poles, nor indeed have I run seven marathons on seven continents within seven consecutive days. My travelling has all happened more or less by accident: things happened to me which made it possible. Ranulph Fiennes is in a class all by himself.

On my first paid day as a member of the British Antarctic Survey I met future colleagues at the Survey's premises in Cambridge and we had the great privilege of meeting the last living member of Scott's last, sad expedition. He was Sir Raymond Priestley, a geologist whose experience was, in some ways, more testing than Scott's. He was in a group of naval personnel and scientists who went round the coast from the main base to Cape Evans where they did geological research. At the end of the summer season, they assembled at the point where the ship was due to pick them up – but it didn't. The pack ice had been blown in and the ship did not even get near enough to take them off, so they faced nine months of loneliness until the following season. Their clothes and tents were worn; their food supply was severely limited; they were a Naval group of officers and other ranks plus scientists, faced with a long hungry wait until rescue could reach them a year later.

Sir Raymond told the story with a cheery bravado which is possible in retrospect but very different in reality. They lived in an ice cave and a line was drawn down the middle of it. On one side was the Officer's Mess and on the other the Other Ranks' Mess, which seems bizarre, but as he explained it, the line did much to preserve their sanity, because the Other Ranks could say whatever they liked about the officers without penalty, as would be the case under normal circumstances, and the Officers "couldn't hear a word". It was a very British solution to a stressful situation.

They ate penguin and seal meat as and when available – and they survived until the ship eventually rescued them the following season. Sir Raymond was the last survivor of Scott's exhibition and I am proud to have shaken his hand. He was eighty-two at the time.

*In 2022 my wife and I went to the new Victoria and Albert Exhibition Centre in Dundee which was built beside Scott's expedition ship 'Discovery'. I had great pleasure in paying my money to see over the ship. It had been built in Dundee for Scott's expedition. I was eighty-two at the time of my visit to the ship and it struck me that I had shaken the hand of that eighty-two-year-old survivor of Scott's expedition. I wrote to the management of the ship explaining that a handshake between two eighty-two-year-old men was a direct link to Scott's expedition. I had a nice letter of acknowledgement from the management of the ship.*

## Preparation for the Job

The job was a radio sonde meteorologist, meaning that every day we took surface observations on temperature, air pressure and humidity. and also sent up a hydrogen balloon with a radio transmitter attached. The signals from the transmitter were then interpreted in terms of pressure, temperature and humidity. The balloon would also be tracked by radar to determine the wind velocity at different heights. There was a three-month training course, first at Hemsby in Norfolk and then in Shetland.

I am so glad I had time in Shetland – before the discovery of oil. Remember, television was in its infancy and many were hostile to the idea of 'bringing the world into your home', as one advertisement put it. There were still ceilidh evenings at the meteorological offices and houses outside Lerwick, where the entertainment and refreshments were all homemade and decidedly better than the offerings on the box. I was invited into a home to watch three or four women doing their knitting Shetland style, namely with a needle in each hand and a third stuck into a sort of leather cushion attached to a belt and that is how you get the astonishing designs on the jerseys that canny fishermen wear. Now, at the time of writing, Shetland means murder-mystery TV programmes in a gloomy landscape.

*22 August 2022: Since writing the above I had the great pleasure, along with more than a thousand other people, of listening to Sir Ranulph Fiennes speaking of his Polar expeditions and I cringe at describing my puny experiences. Within the geographical context my part of Antarctica, Grahamland, or 'the Antarctic Peninsula, south of Cape Horn', is humorously called 'the banana belt', since the temperature there rarely fell below –40 degrees!*

The climax of my training was to be on the dock at Southampton one day in December 1961 along with about twenty other men around my age. Sir Vivian Fuchs, the Director, turned up to say farewell, driving a brand, new Jaguar E Type. These were my kind of people! He was persuaded, without much difficulty, to raise the bonnet on a V12 engine, if I remember rightly. The journey south was memorable for several reasons, the worst being three prostrate days of sea-sickness in the cabin as the RMS Kista Dan, a Danish ship adapted for work in polar regions, wallowed its way through the Bay of Biscay, but by the time we reached the Falklands that was a distant memory.

A little political background is necessary here. In the late 19th century various countries laid claim to segments of the Antarctic continent. Britain claimed a large wedge of Antarctica south of Cape Horn at the tip of South America on the grounds of our possession of the Falkland Islands. Famously, the ownership of the Falklands later became hotly contested by Argentina, but originally Britain needed coaling stations placed strategically round the world to service the Royal Navy, and the few inhabitants on the islands were in no position to argue. All that would come later.

In due course both Argentina and Chile claimed over-lapping segments in the same area and that was the situation in 1961, with sometimes comic results. For example, there was a famous base on Deception Island, which was the partly submerged crater of an extinct, well nearly extinct, volcano. The warmed beaches steamed gently in all weathers. Ships could get in by a very narrow entrance into a wide bay which was the submerged core of the old volcano, but this ideal location was also claimed by Argentina and Chile. When we anchored by our base, a small boat left each of the other bases bearing the leaders, who arrived armed with indignant letters along the lines of,

> The President and Parliament of Chile note with alarm
> the presence of a British ship in Chilean waters without
> the prior consent of the Chilean Government

and a similar letter was presented by the Argentinian Captain. We Brits had a small pile of similar letters in return, whereupon the drinks came out and there was bonhomie all round.

However, in 1957 there was a moratorium on all claims in the interests of international cooperation, particularly during a 'Geo-physical Year' in 1957. So, I was employed by the Falkland Islands Dependencies Survey and employees were known as FIDS for short. A year later we became the British Antarctic Survey, so the Governor of the Falkland Islands now had two territories, namely the Falklands and the Antarctic Territories, and therefore two salaries. That is how these things are done!

## South from the Falklands

All the incoming FIDS were invited to a reception at Government House, in Port Stanley, which was my introduction to the little rituals of the Foreign Service. Each of the new arrivals lined up to shake the hands of the Governor and his Lady before drinks were served and we milled around. I was most impressed that he knew each one of us by name when introduced ("Aaah, it is Kimber, isn't it?) which showed that he had a very good memory for faces and had spent a good deal of time studying our photographs before the reception. Then quite suddenly there were the Governor and his wife standing by the door which meant, 'Time to go'. I later found that this is the ritual Foreign Office custom all over the world.

From the Falklands we had a leisurely journey south, visiting the northerly bases and cooperating with the Navy to do seismic surveys in the South Shetland Islands, but then we were steaming down the most dramatic coastline I had ever seen, through light pack ice, with vertical, ice-bound cliffs on the port side and a chaotic jumble of bergs on the starboard. This was Le Maire Channel which steadily narrowed until we dropped anchor in the sheltered bay and the base called Port Locroy. For some reason which I never discovered, it had a Post Office whose postmaster was the leader of a small FIDS base doing geo-physical research and selling stamps for letters home from the most southerly post office in the world (I think).

From there we finally burst out into a wide sea covered with broken ice and bergs as far as the eye could see, and on our port side the continuing spine of the Grahamland Peninsula. It was a magnificent spectacle as glaciers poured down the valleys between jagged frozen peaks. We approached a cluster of small islands, one of which was my Base, the Argentine Islands. The name sounded like a surrender to the territorial claims of our South American rivals (see above) but their discovery predated international rivalry for the territory.

This was to be home for two years. There was a lot of bustle as we unloaded the cargo; met the outgoing Fids and were welcomed by the few remainers. Two months later the RMS Shackleton paid its final visit; we sent last letters to loved ones and that was that for the next nine months.

I will never forget my first day on our small island. It had a permanent ice-cap rising to about 300 feet. Beyond, lay five miles of sea, then covered intermittently with ice floes which would soon freeze into solid sea ice. I stood on the top and looked across to the mainland: just white cliffs, glaciers, peaks and valleys as far as the eye could see north and south, The sky was, unusually, calm with a scattering of pink, woolly alto-cumulus clouds as the sun sank slowly below the horizon. But everything was silent. Everything! There was no noise from the base; there was no wind; there was none of the usual crunch and slurp of ice floes moving with the tide. Nothing. For maybe twenty minutes I stood and listened – to nothing – until at last there came the loneliest sound you could imagine: the first pathetic bleat of a new-born seal between birth and suckling. In all that majestic panorama there was no other sound.

*Politics and religion. There was no formal statement about the personal convictions of personnel but it was understood that religion and politics were personal matters and were not discussed. One colleague was a Roman Catholic and I was an Evangelical. I had a couple of theology books on the shelf by my bed and I read my Bible daily, but this was presumably noted without comment.*

## The People

Most FIDS had a lot in common, like irresponsibility, a desire to avoid a steady job, a passion for outdoors and many had considerable mountaineering experience, some of them to a very high standard indeed. Some were professional scientists while others, like me, had trained specifically for the job. My base was a small, ice-capped island five miles off the western coast of the Antarctic or Grahamland Peninsula if you are British, south of Cape Horn. A dozen of us shared the hut, which was heated with anthracite coal. This may seem antiquated but was in fact the most efficient form of transportable energy, brought in canvas bags and unloaded by hand – like everything else.

We had a cook, who worked five days a week, and we shared the weekend cooking, two at a time, which produced a sort of undeclared rivalry to see who could produce the best grub and particularly fresh bread and rolls every other day. In our first year the cook had been a pâtissier at the Savoy hotel in London and on festive occasions he could produce some spectacular offerings, but also the occasional burst of professional neurosis. On one occasion, after a poor day's cooking, there was a hole lower down in the plasterboard wall of the kitchen which perfectly matched the cook's size nine shoe. That cook (sorry: chef) decided that one year was enough and returned home to be replaced by another less distinguished chef (or cook) who decided that the summer weather predicted a winter rather more bleak than he expected and took the last boat home. I can't remember how we solved the problem, but I suspect that we took it a week at a time.

Four of us were Met men: there were two ionosphericists, a general duties bod, a diesel mechanic, an RAF radar operator, and a radio operator. Every day we Met men made hydrogen to fill a large balloon, as follows. First, we filled what looked like a large milk churn with a mixture of aluminium filings and anhydrous sodium hydroxide. This was put into the lower chamber of a generator which had an upper chamber filled with water. (Work out the chemistry yourself). Of course, all water had to be made by melting snow, which was a slow and painful process. When water was added to the mixed chemicals below, hydrogen was emitted and passed into the balloon.

This sounds beguilingly simple. It took place in a large shed with slatted doors so that the balloon could emerge through the down-wind door. The balloon had attached to it 100 feet of string and then a radio transmitter which, ideally, ascended into the heavens emitting a stream of signals which were interpreted as measures of temperature, pressure and humidity. However, when the wind could reach more than 100 knots on occasions it was much more likely that the balloon would take off horizontally, smashing the transmitter to smithereens. Then the process was repeated.

The transmitter was a strange looking object; like a round carboard bucket with a child's windmill attached. In the bucket were three sensors, one measuring temperature, one humidity and one air pressure. The windmill, as it rotated, switched on one of these three sensors in turn and transmitted a signal which was picked up on an oscilloscope on the ground. The job of the operator was to produce a signal with a frequency equal to the incoming one and plot it on a piece of graph paper. This information would be turned into statements of pressure, temperature and humidity as the balloon rose until it eventually burst. Many thousands of these primitive machines are scattered far and wide across Antarctica.

Nearby, George, the radar operator, was sitting in his mobile cabin, picking up an echo from a piece of aluminium foil attached to the balloon and plotting the altitude and bearing of the balloon as it soared heavenwards, until it reached the stratosphere – and burst.

And finally, sitting cosily in the base hut and stroking the expeditionary cat, was Charlie, the radio operator, reading a novel until all the processes were complete, when, with a yawn, he would transmit the day's data by morse code, to another cosy operator in the Falkland Islands who forwarded data from all the British bases to an international centre where all data were collated.

At every stage of this daily activity there were opportunities for failure, but with practice failure was infrequent. Our primitive equipment was at that time about to be replaced with computerised processes for receiving and interpreting data. We were at the end of an era. In parallel with the radio sonde procedures, surface information was collected by traditional methods in all weathers in the standard Stevenson screens. Reading a thermometer every three hours in a blizzard and winds which did reach a hundred knots on occasions, required a lot of warm clothing and a sort of dogged stubbornness.

Finally, in my second year the ionosphericists asked me to operate an ozone spectro-photometer to relieve them of some work. As a background to this work, the following quotation from Ranulph Fiennes' book describes the problem:

> Man-made pollutants called chloro-fluorocarbons are released from aerosols and coolants in the cold and dark of the Antarctic winter. As the sun returns in spring, these frozen chemicals react with the sun's rays, releasing chlorine molecules that temporarily dissolve the thin layer of ozone that protects earth-bound life on earth below." (page 164)

The terrestrial effects of this upper-atmospheric chemistry included sheep in Patagonia which went blind because the depleted ozone layer allowed destructive radiation to damage the retina of sheep's eyes.

In my last year I took over responsibility for the spectro-photometer which took daily readings of the state of the ozone layer. These readings were accumulated with others from around the world and finally identified the problem. Solving it was much more difficult. Persuading manufacturers around the world that the damage done in the atmosphere affects more than Patagonian sheep, was much more difficult.

My part in this research was infinitesimally small.

# Huskies

We probably had the last usable huskies on our base, and it was more an act of kindness, than any practical use they might provide, that we fed them daily on seal meat, but their eagerness to be useful was worthy of a retirement home for Normandy veterans. Two things galvanised them: food and anything that looked like a sledge (and, I suppose, sex). One of the Met men took them to his heart, and you could smell him at twenty yards. There is something unique about rancid blubber that is a warning to the squeamish. Tony Schärer didn't actually volunteer to care for the dogs: he just did it and none of us chose to argue the point. Tony had Swiss ancestors so before publication I couldn't spell his name properly because my keyboard has no umlaut – those two little dots above the 'a' in his surname that make his name rhyme with 'fairer'. For short he was just called 'Umlaut'!

The dog job had two parts: getting the food and storing enough for the winter, and then feeding the dogs daily. They spent much of their lives chained to a long cable so that their own private feuds could not be fulfilled – until they were attached to a sledge and then the two bitches started the fight (simply what happened – not in the least a sexist comment). Greta and Roo simply lived to hate and fight because each had been a lead dog – the fight showed who was boss. But first the matter of food.

Our colleagues who lived on bases further south rudely referred to our base as the 'banana belt' and in relative terms that is fair, because we were the third furthest north and we had good open water at the height of summer. The marine wildlife lived on krill, those small shrimp-like creatures which multiply in astronomical numbers and are the main food of penguins and all marine mammals. As chance would have it our little archipelago surrounded a natural harbour which was accessible for our small ships and also somnolent seals. Umlaut would scan the bay every morning in summer for ice floes which occasionally had a sleeping seal on board, stuffed to the eyeballs with krill, whereupon Umlaut and another would row gently out to the floe and put a bullet just behind the seal's ear and there was enough food for the dogs for a couple of months – but first it had to be stored underneath a tarpaulin for as long as possible until the blubber was rancid enough to be discerned at fifty yards in a gentle breeze.

Feeding time was bedlam. As soon as Umlaut raised the tarpaulin from the carcasses every dog started yelling until a big glob of stinking blubber appeared. Then peace reigned as eight bloated bellies set to with the digestion.

Strictly speaking the dogs were superfluous because we were a static base and a couple of other bases had teams going out to geologise or do surveying, but they had finally been equipped with motorised transport of various kinds, including one that was fun but useless. It was a tin cabin on skis with a small aero engine and propeller behind. More sophisticated vehicles were used widely. So, the dogs were, if you like, a luxury and had been spared, first because no one had the heart to shoot them and secondly, we did use them for exercise and when we went on trips for work or recreation. Let me describe a typical scenario.

Elsewhere I have described a holiday I took with Chips Vickerstaff and Andy Mack so let me bring the dogs into the cast. Wild excitement when the sledge appears, particularly between Roo and Greta: this is a status thing. Whichever is chosen will have a fight as soon as the sledge moves and progress is impossible until this is sorted out either by a human or by all the other dogs having their say – with their teeth. It was quickest just to accept the canine solution rather than interfere at this stage. Human control had its place eventually (we are the master race after all) but why spoil the fun?

Useful progress of any distance really depended on Eddie. I almost well up when I think of Eddie: always at the back of the team doing 90% of the pulling, rather like the horse in Animal Farm who constantly said, " I . . . must . . . work . . . harder!" Being at the back of the team and nearest the sledge he should have been able to see that all the rest were slacking and doing little more than keeping the traces straight while bickering and gossiping went on among the fairer sex.

Umlaut was very conscientious about exercising the dogs, but space was limited in the summer when the sea ice had broken up; however, once the sea ice froze it was great to see the sledge and the dogs in use. The price to pay for a sledge trip, was the process outlined above – except to add that this process was always accompanied by wild yells of excitement throughout. The temptation to say, "maybe tomorrow . . ." was strong.

Umlaut was a quiet chap, but once when the tongue got loosened, he told us how he had bought a small barrel of pickled herrings in Helsinki to take to his grandmother who lived on the Atlantic coast of Norway, but for some reason he never explained, he chose to take a coastal boat right up the gulf of Bothnia where he took a train to northern Norway and thence by a coastal mail boat that took him, via every small harbour on the Atlantic coast, to southern Norway where his grandmother lived and he could deliver the pickled herrings she loved. There must have been an easier way. With him there was no reason to doubt the truth of it. It sort of went with a man who fed huskies and shared the smell.

## Alarms and Excursions

I had a few near disasters, some unavoidable and at least one as the result of sheer stupidity, which might well have ended in a fatality. As previously mentioned, the base was on a small island five miles off the mainland. Base rules said that no-one should go further than 400 yards from the base alone without a sledge carrying a tent and sufficient rations for ten days. There were good reasons for this although I never saw this admirable safety rule put into practice. Although we could have long periods of high pressure system with calm weather, things could occasionally turn violent without warming and temperature could drop twenty degrees in a few minutes accompanied by a furious wind.

In addition, the sea ice could and did break up on occasions, and with an off-shore gale could produce open water. In fact, a few years previously two men and a dog team were lost in this way and since then the same has happened elsewhere. However, quite soon after the sea froze, I had some spare time so decided to cross to the mainland, five miles away, to take photos up on a glacier. It was a beautiful Autumn day; what could possibly go wrong, and I returned unscathed a few hours later. It was a trip we often took for a day's climbing.

But the result was quite different in my first Spring. On a clear, calm afternoon, I again crossed the ice along with George, the radar mechanic. George was new to skis and for some reason his kept falling off, which meant that he was very delayed. Daylight was limited and by the time we reached the mainland the sun was setting. As we crossed the ice en-route for home, George got slower and slower and then stopped. I kept urging him to keep going because the temperature was in the −20s. Eventually when the base was in sight, I told him not to stop and I set off for base to get help. I explained what had happened; we got a sledge plus blankets and hot water bottles and retraced my ski tracks until we could see George – lying prone on the snow. It was a very nasty moment. We got him on the sledge with blankets and hot bottles and into the base. After some very violent shivering for an hour or so, he settled down and was OK.

However, in the post-mortem (metaphorical sense) we could all see the necessity for strict discipline about leaving base. George's problem was, first of all, his skis. It was their malfunction which held us up and my nagging didn't help. Secondly, his collapse was probably the result of sheer fear because he was a very strong lad who later did much more skiing without any problem. It had been a very calm, cold day with a low sun, but in dusk and then darkness, the pale sea ice, which creaks and groans as you move, becomes eerie. The silent immensity is either thrilling or terrifying, depending on circumstances. Whatever the reason for George's collapse, he was none the worse next day and we had lots of longer trips later.

Another anxious event came in my first holiday. We were entitled to a two-week break which could be spent any way we wished – within limits. Two of my friends and I took the dog sledge, well loaded with a tent and plenty of fuel and food, for a trip down south of the base over the sea ice. The weather was fine, and we travelled about twenty miles on the first day. There is an absolute rule that you don't ever camp on sea ice.

With this solemn reminder we set out across a very wide bay some miles off-shore and kept a look-out for a suitable camping sight, but the best we could find before nightfall was a rock standing about three feet above the ice with enough space to set up the tent with the dogs tethered partly on the rock and the rest on the sea ice.

Camping is a slow painful process involving setting up the tent securely and then laying out three sleeping spaces inside, plus space for two boxes, one carrying food for ten man-days and the other a primus stove and cooking equipment. We each slept on a blown-up lilo with a sheepskin on it and then a double sleeping bag. That, with the heat from the primus stove kept you warm until the small hours of the night. However, in those same small hours an off-shore blizzard with strong, gale-force wind began, which lasted for thirty-six hours. It is difficult to rehearse the mental processes of lying virtually imprisoned in a tent as the wind batters the fabric relentlessly, hour after hour. I think each of us had in mind the fate of the two men and the dog team who were lost when the pack ice broke up.

The sound of tent walls endlessly flapping becomes psychologically destructive. When it died down, a day and a half later, we saw that all the ice to sea-ward of us had blown out of sight leaving unbroken open water. To landward, the ice was still fast, giving us time to pack up, hitch up the dogs and head north again before the ice broke up during the next big blizzard.

"My God, that was lucky," said Andy. "Thank God for praying parents," was my reaction. Indeed, all my family were active Christians and I knew that my parents, if not all my siblings, would remember me in their daily devotions. Does prayer make a difference?

Let me give you another similar story which I can absolutely vouch for and the details are recorded in Sir Vivian Fuchs' book about BAS, called *Of Ice and Men*. Moreover Bob Metcalf, who told me the story, was the central character in the event which took place two years before my own story above and like me was a practising Christian.

Briefly, two teams of scientists with support personnel were travelling across a large area of sea ice, with tractor-drawn sledges. They had no choice but to camp on sea ice for at least forty-eight hours while a full gale blew constantly. In the middle of the second night they realised that they were moving as cracks opened up in several places, including the floor of Bob's tent. As Bob told it to me, at one stage in the darkness he 'saw' in his mind's eye what looked like a notice board with on it the words, "Oh you of little faith; why do you doubt?" namely the words of Jesus to his disciples in a storm at sea. He shared this confidence with some of the team and faced a very natural scepticism. However, when day finally broke, they found that their teams were all on a large floe which had rammed itself onto a beach. There was time enough for everyone to get onto the land with all the equipment, after which the floe which bore them drifted away. The teams waited until the sea froze over sufficiently and then drove back to base.

## Mount Balch

My next holiday was indeed spent on land and it had alarms of a different kind. There are, somewhere, slides of the base where we lived with the mainland five miles away. It is a stunning location. The Antarctic Peninsula lay five miles to the east of us and it is a series of mountains and sheer cliffs with glaciers pouring down from an inland plateau to the sea. The highest adjacent point was Mount Balch, about 4,000 feet, and there is no record of it having been climbed before, so this was the goal for two friends and me. Bob Lewis was the only serious climber but Pete Blakely and I were up for it, so we loaded a sledge for a trip across the sea ice, up a glacier onto a plateau which left a climb of about 1500 feet to the top.

It was a real struggle up the glacier, with deep snow to wade through and significant crevassing to avoid. We camped on a level bit of glacier and well clear of a steep ice cliff which calved periodically through the days and nights with a thunderous roar while we were there. Camping food lacked sophistication and imagination. It came in boxes containing 10 man-days of supplies, all of it either dried or canned. Usually this meant stew in one form or another which was boiled up with snow and served with reconstituted dried potato and half a pound of butter dropped in when everything was boiling happily.

The climb to the top was tricky with intervals of soft snow, rock, bare ice and steep climbs over these varying surfaces. The worst bit was something I had not met before but had prepared for. It was a steep, near vertical ice cliff that needed crampons, ice axes to cut steps and tethered ropes while we climbed the worst bits one at a time. I have clear memories of looking down between my feet with almost two thousand feet of a potential fall below. The worst bit was coming down the same pitch facing outwards.

The happy conclusion was that the other two told me to face the wall of the tent, lie down with a book and leave them to make the meal which turned out to be a birthday meal – for I had forgotten that the date was indeed 3 September 1963 (being pre-occupied with other matters – like staying alive). They had brought along dehydrated steaks and potatoes, a frozen bottle of red wine and a Christmas pudding. A perfect celebration for my first serious climb.

As I was finishing writing this in April 2022, I remembered this climb and wondered if it really was a first ascent, so I wrote to the British Antarctic Survey and received a very friendly letter and a copy of the report which Bob Lewis had submitted. In brief, it was indeed a first ascent. For those who are interested in these things, in an Appendix at the back is a copy of the report sent to British Antarctic Survey HQ.

## Midwinter

The Polar year turned on mid-winter's day, the 21$^{st}$ of June or thereabouts, with a modest party. We had large quantities of alcohol and 140,000 cigarettes in stock, but no-one got drunk and most people who came as smokers went back cured – until the boat arrived and once at sea many of the smokers started again. It defied logic.

There was a tradition that anyone who told the same joke or story more than once had their name added to a list on the wall of the mess, but while the story was being told, everyone listened solemnly to the end – and then the name went up on the wall. However, on my second mid-winter the conversation turned on what lay ahead for those of us whose two years would end around Christmas time 1963 and one of the wilder ideas centred on the Island of South Georgia and the 1964 Olympics in Tokyo.

The link between them was the closure of Salvesen's whaling operations in South Georgia and the news that some of the whaling ships would be left to rot there, since it was uneconomic to sail them home for scrap. Gradually an idea formed around getting one of these boats and sailing it to Japan, and in fact we got as far as sending a telegram to Salvesen's asking if we could have a boat and the answer was very clear: if you can get there you can have it. The Survey's boat, RMS Shackleton, made at least a couple of trips to South Georgia during the summer, so there was a good chance we could hitch a ride.

So, what could we do with the ship? At that time our annual salaries were £500 p.a. all found and most of us were happy to put one year's pay into a kitty. Where could we get fuel? Hopefully there was enough left in South Georgia to get as far as Punta Arenas in the Straits of Magellan. What about food? We had an emergency hut with several year's food which needed to be replenished and we could live on that for a Pacific crossing. Who would work the ship? Our diesel mechanic was a genius with diesels and on the basis of my navigator's wings I thought I could aim for Japan.

All this was enough encouragement to make more detailed inquiries. What size were the engines? What make were they? How much fuel did they use? Were the ships in reasonable working order? Would the Survey take us to South Georgia? Could we get the right maps? All these questions were fired off to Salvesen's and while we waited the next question was, "How do we get home from Japan?" I favoured going to Vladivostok in Russia and then travelling home by the trans-Siberian railway.

And then the bad news (or maybe it was the good news): the ship's engines generated 2,000 horse-power and needed a river of diesel oil every hour. We could make it about half way across the Pacific. So died the mid-winter dream. But it left me with the same problem: how should I go home? I could just sit on the last Survey ship that took the lads to waiting fiancées or girlfriends, but I had no such pressures – so then the obvious answer was to go to Montreal where brother Ashley and sister Joyce were living. I could leave the boat in Montevideo, Uruguay, and find my way through Argentina, Paraguay, Brazil, Bolivia, Peru, and so on through central

America to Mexico and the USA to Canada, and that is what I did. Ideally, I should have learnt Spanish with enough of it to survive, but there were no teach-yourself books to do that. I was sure I could get by.

The second great idea was to get from my parents and friends the names of anyone they knew in South and Central America and that is what happened: I sponged off them!

In January 1964 the Shackleton pulled away from Base F leaving the hut that had been a very happy home for two years. Instead of sailing direct to the Falklands, the skipper fabricated an excuse to go to Punta Arenas in the Southern tip of Chile on the Straits of Magellan. There are easy ways to make this journey and there are others which demand a high degree of seamanship and favourable weather. We had both. Cape Horn, of fearsome reputation, was flat calm, so we sailed round it and up the Beagle Channel, so called after the ship on which Charles Darwin famously travelled en route for the Galapagos Islands and *The Origin of Species*. It was an epic journey at very slow speeds.

Later I read a famous book about Tierra del Fuego called *The Uttermost Parts of the Earth*. Ironically, Darwin decided that the natives of Td F were a sub-human species of anthropoids which were trapped in an earlier stage of evolution. However, *The Uttermost Parts of the Earth* was written by a missionary who took a very different view of the same natives. He and his family lived there for many years and found them to be primitive but every bit as human as the rest of us.

We stopped to refuel in Punta Arenas in the Straits of Magellan and at that time it still had relics of British influence in the form of a gentlemen's club with brown leather armchairs and pictures of long-dead Chairmen. Britain's ambition to 'rule the waves' with the Falklands as a vital coaling station, meant that a presence of some kind was necessary in this vital area where Chile and Argentina came together.

Many years later I read the best book about sailing ever written. I refer, of course, to Joshua Slocum's *Sailing Alone Around the World*. Slocum's background was in the whaling ports of America so he knew the South Atlantic well. He decided that he wanted to be the first man to 'sail alone around the world' and did it in a boat which he built himself. His adventures in the Straits of Magellan tied in with Darwin's experience with the natives of Tierra del Fuego. When he stopped in Punta Arenas and explained the aim of his voyage, he was warned against the natives who, he was assured, were evil thieves who should be shot on sight, since they would board his boat and steal every moveable object. However, Slocum had a better plan that enabled him to sleep easily. He moored in a suitable inlet and bedded down for the night until he was woken by screams of pain from the deck. When he got up, he saw several of the locals dancing and screaming – as they trod on the tin tacks which he had scattered liberally on deck. No lives were lost.

A final memory of Slocum's journey was his problem explaining his voyage to the Prime Minister of South Africa who firmly believed that the world was flat.

## Postscript

There is an interesting sequel to the South Georgia story. Many years later I got to know Alistair Salvesen, a Director of the Christian-Salvesen group of companies, who lives just a few miles from us. I told him about our abortive attempt to reach the Tokyo Olympics. He remembered my request and said that the old whaling ships and much other ironmongery still lie in South Georgia to this day, but in 1982 he had been approached by an Argentinian scrap metal dealer who wanted to buy all the scrap metal, including the boats. Permission was given and the scrap merchant was the cover for the Argentinian invasion of South Georgia and the Falklands.

The sequel to that story was that the same Argentinian dealer had applied yet again to buy the scrap metal. Alistair gave him permission and added that since the previous time there was now a great deal more scrap metal, in the shape of military hardware, than the last time.

Base F had been a happy home for two memorable years. There was no violence apart from a minor skirmish between Andy and the cook (sorry – chef) but that is the artistic temperament for you.

I kept in touch with a few friends in a desultory way. I was a guest at Chips Vickerstaff's wedding before he was appointed transport manager of a diamond mine in South Africa and he set off to drive there, Sahara Desert, wife and unborn child notwithstanding. Years later I had a mysterious communication from a Professor (?) Andrew Mack from a university in British Columbia. It was too late to warn the authorities about such an outrageous appointment.

For myself, I decided to take 'The Long Way Home' – via South, Central and North America and Iceland back to Scotland.

# Chapter 4 The Americas

## Uruguay and Argentina

So, there I was on the dock in Montevideo, Uruguay, waving goodbye to the RRS Shackleton and my erstwhile friends. I had contacted missionaries whose names had been given to me and they entertained me royally for a few days while I bought travellers' cheques in US dollars and took advice about the way ahead, including the suggestion that the best way to travel cheaply in the USA was to buy a Greyhound bus ticket at $99 for 99 days anywhere in the USA or Canada. I offered to take my hosts out for a meal by way of thanks and asked for a typical Uruguayan meal: 'Pizza!' Post-war South America was flooded with refugees from all over Europe, but mainly Italy.

The best way to Argentina, apparently, was by bus, west along the coast to a point where a hydro-foil crossed the Rio del Plata to Buenos Aires in Argentina.

*While crossing the River Plate estuary I couldn't help wondering if we were sailing over the wreck of the German battleship 'Graf Spee' which was badly wounded in December 1939 by two British Cruisers. The Captain of the Graf Spee asked if the fuel tanks of his ship could be repaired in Montevideo. The reply was that he could have only three days or Uruguay's neutrality would be compromised. Thinking that a large British fleet awaited him in the open Atlantic, he scuttled his ship in the estuary of the river Plate. In fact only two cruisers were waiting for him, though reinforcements were on the way.*

I had the name of a family called the Lears, old friends of my parents. I walked up from the harbour to the city centre with all my worldly goods in a large rucksack and a camera bag. I phoned the Lears: no answer. I tried again later with the same result. It was getting later so I checked into a cheap hotel and tried again. No luck. Next day I took a walk round the area and came across a Christian bookshop. I went in and asked, in very fractured Spanish, if the shop-keeper knew the Lears. "Si Si!" He had as much English as I had Spanish. However, a man who was glancing at a book overheard and said, "Yes, I know the Lears. They live near me but they are out of town for a week. Come and stay with me: I have a flat nearby."

My host, Jim Fry, was a British business man who had lived in Argentina for many years and I was made welcome in his bachelor flat. Then he apologised that he would have to leave me in order to give away the bride at a wedding in the absence of her father. "However," he said, "I have just phoned the Lears' daughter and she would be delighted to entertain you while I am at the wedding," and that is what happened. I had a meal with Mrs Lear Junior until Jim Fry unexpectedly returned and said that the bridegroom's father, in whose grounds the wedding was held, came from Aberdeen and demanded that I should go to the reception and tell him about Aberdeen, so I did.

I can't remember the name of the bridegroom's father, but he was geniality itself. He had migrated to Argentina from Aberdeen in the 1930 depression and had eventually done very well, importing agricultural machinery and then he said, "I can only remember the name of one friend in Aberdeen: his name was Alfie Cordiner," so I was happy to say that my sister was married to Alfie's brother. The floodgates of hospitality were flung open and I was introduced to a little group of exiled Scots who were getting maudlin in a corner of the marquee. As time passed they launched into 'The Northern Lights of Old Aberdeen' in honour of my appearance and the ancient roots of our host, who had done well out of Argentinian farmers – as any Aberdonian would have done.

The hospitality got better. Next morning my host asked if I rowed and I assumed that he wasn't talking about a rowing boat round the harbour. I was right and he took me to a splendid Rowing Club on the grassy banks of the Parana river. It was an old men's eight and they graciously allowed me to demonstrate the limited skills I had acquired in a summer term's rowing in Oxford. It was a reminder of more affluent times when most of the financial investment in Argentina came from Britain, but sadly most of these had been liquidated to pay for the first and second world wars. None the less there was an Edwardian graciousness about it all. My host was very kind and indeed that was true of everyone I met. I suppose my Antarctic stories did me no harm.

## Asuncion – Paraguay

I would have loved to travel up the Parana and Paraguay rivers to Asuncion, the capital, but the rivers were low and it would have taken a couple of weeks at the best of times, so I flew. Again, the old Christian missionary network turned up trumps. When my brother Ashley was a baby, my parents met a couple of newly-weds called Mr and Mrs Tait. It is hard to believe, but they were so impressed with Ashley that they called their first-born Ashley. I had contacted them, and they met me at the airport. I was royally entertained for a few days and it was there I ate my first avocado. Over a period of twenty years or more they had built up a small church and this included a river boat in which members of their church made evangelistic forays up the Paraguay river.

General Stroessner had been the President since 1954 and his reign lasted for 35 years. Through it all he gave refuge to a nasty selection of deposed, renegade Latin American and other Presidents who ran out of luck, not to mention notorious Nazi refugees like Martin Borman and the infamous Doctor Mengele, the doctor of death, who experimented on innumerable concentration camp victims.

I discussed with the Taits how to make my way north and they were very practical. The best people to buy tickets were the Mennonites, a Christian group which developed during the Reformation when Christians broke away from the Catholic Church and, in many cases, endured persecution in their native land and settled in many parts of the Americas. From my point of view, they ran excellent travel agencies, where I got a ticket for a flight to Campo Grande, Brazil, in a small plane in which I was the sole passenger. It could be dangerously habit-forming.

I have a weakness for minority religious movements, on the basis that majorities are usually wrong, and the Mennonites are an interesting example of people who in the 16th century were part of the Reformation. They were typical of various kinds of Baptists who took the view that personal faith should be a conscious, adult decision to be marked by a public statement of faith solemnised by baptism, preferably by immersion, in line with John the Baptist's practice. Typically, they were persecuted and emigrated, some to Ukraine, where we will encounter them later in this book, and later to various parts of the Americas. More to the point, they were excellent business people and first-rate travel agents. who would transfer money honestly and cheaply to anywhere in the world through their own networks.

*Here is a sample of their beliefs:*

*In the Mennonite heritage, these beliefs lead to distinctive emphases.*
*Faith is voluntary.*
*Christians are called to a life of love, reconciliation and peace-making.*
*Injustice is to be overcome with good.*
*Happiness is more than material well-being.*
*Moral authority is more than political power.*
*Life is to be lived simply.*
*All of nature is a gift of God to be cherished with a sense of gratitude and*
*stewardship.*
*Loving, sacrificial service is the highest expression of faithfulness to Christ.*

Paraguay seems a crazy country. At different times it has fought all its neighbours: Argentina, Brazil, Bolivia together and separately. At one stage a third of the male population died in defence of a worthless tract of unproductive land called the Chaco.

## Brazil: Campo Grande and Corumba

I had no preferred route from Montevideo to Montreal. I had warned the family that they probably wouldn't get much news from me because by the time a post card reached Aberdeen from lowland Bolivia or the highlands of Ecuador, I would be somewhere else but there was no cause for concern and so it turned out. I flew in a small plane from Paraguay to Campo Grande in the Mato Grosso of Brazil. Who did I know in Campo Grande? No one, but the Taits did and they kindly contacted American friends in Campo Grande who gave me a bed for the night in exchange for news from Antarctica. I got the impression that not a lot happens in Campo Grande, despite the name. The value of the US dollar against whatever the currency of Brazil was at that time meant that I travelled for a whole day first class on a fine train for the equivalent of about $1.50. The end of that journey was the town of Corumba on the banks of the river Paraguay and the problem was where next and how to get there.

Across the river was lowland Bolivia but there were no scheduled flights and no boats. Everyone had warned me to carry a gun and indeed I was just falling asleep in a cheap hotel when about midnight there were six shots outside my window. At breakfast I asked who had died but apparently it was just the parish priest calling the faithful to midnight mass on Good Friday.

49

While I hung around trying to get across to Bolivia I fell in with an extraordinary man. He was an Estonian whose country had successively been over-run first by the Germans and then the Russians in WW2. To escape the Russians, whom he feared and hated, he walked across the winter ice of the Baltic Sea to Sweden and then fled from Sweden when the Russians demanded the repatriation of Estonian refugees. Without money and passport, he fled across war-desolated Europe seeking any country that would accept him as a refugee. France was his last refuge, but in constant fear of Russia in 1946/47 he applied for a visa to Argentina and got one. When I met him, he was travelling, again without visa and apparently without money, to the USA to sell beryllium to the steel industry. (Don't try to make sense of this: he lived in a world I could not imagine. He thought my modest spending on food and lodging was irresponsibly prodigal,)

## Bolivia: Santa Cruz and La Paz

He introduced me to an American pilot and owner of a mysterious Dakota plane that was due to fly into Bolivia that evening and so it happened. I shared the hold with strange packages covered with a net and the pilot found me a seat and screwed it into the floor. The flight to the town of Santa Cruz was fairly short, but when we landed, he circled the perimeter of the airfield rather than taxiing straight to the shack that served as a terminal building. As we taxied past the encircling jungle, small jeeps emerged and picked up various packages which were thrown out of the plane by the co-pilot. At every stage of the journey through Bolivia there was smuggling. The Government placed road blocks at intervals along the roads to enable police to search passengers and luggage for drugs and other forbidden items, so there would be frantic scurrying to secrete objects under seats or clothing before the cops could get going.

The next stage was to climb from lowland Bolivia to the altiplano – the high plateau between ten and fourteen thousand feet in the Andes. It was a memorable bus ride. At one point we went above 17,000 feet. The local buses were made in Czechoslovakia with very short wheel-bases and therefore long bits of the bus at the front and back, which hung out when taking a corner. Foolishly, I chose to sit at the very front of the bus so that on several occasions I remember looking straight down a sheer cliff to the valley below. One time the driver pointed to a red dot far below which was a local bus that had gone just too close to the edge.

I have been to Bolivia twice, with a twenty-five year gap between visits, and the change was astonishing. To reach La Paz, the capital, you travel for miles across the altiplano, which, as the name suggests is a vast plane at an average of about 10,000 feet above sea level. It is rather featureless until quite suddenly you arrive at the edge of a huge crater, in which is La Paz, the capital. The city centre is at the bottom of the crater and suburbs of diminishing prosperity climb the walls. At least that is my memory from the first visit. The second time, in 1989, the population had exploded and the crater had overflowed on to the altiplano to provide space for new housing, which meant that as and when people found some land and a few bags of concrete and steel rods, they would start to build a home, leaving raw edges and spikes for the next time they had a few pesos/escudos/ reals or whatever the currency was called at a particular time.

In most places I had a contact, sometimes to a missionary or just a friend of the last place I stayed. Ken Jones was my kind host in La Paz and my abiding memory was a Sunday service in a house at the top of the crater where a small congregation gathered in a slum dwelling not many yards from the rubbish tip which was also the public toilet – or lack of it – yet I will always remember a communion service with illiterate, poverty-stricken people and smiling faces – and I never understood a word.

## Peru: Machu Picchu and Lima

You get to Peru from La Paz by boat and train: yes, a boat at 12,000 feet, to cross Lake Titicaca, and not just a boat but a sailing boat, or more accurately, a wind-driven ferry carrying a bus. Beyond that is a railway station that took me to Cuzco en route for Machu Picchu. In 1964 this was a quiet, beautiful journey by train down a long valley of the Urubamba river and then by a series of tight hairpin bends up to the place itself. Nothing can adequately prepare you for what you see, and I am so glad that I went before tourism overwhelmed it with everything tourists do to a place.

In 1964 I had it almost to myself. The site was discovered only in 1920 by an American archaeologist called Hiram Bingham. Even though the Conquistadors had travelled up and down the trail that runs beside the Urubamba, they never found the 'city' on top of the ridge around which the river curves. When Bingham found it, everything was covered with vegetation but as that was cleared, there were stone terraces with houses and irrigation channels bringing water to every house. But the most striking feature is the view over the valley to the mountains and even more, there was a final pinnacle at the end of the ridge, accessible only by a precipitous, winding path to a few small terraces at the top. From there, there is only a three-thousand-foot sheer dropdown to the valley below. In all directions the mountains roll away, peak after peak into the fading distance.

I climbed to the top. Not many places are awe-some but in the best sense of the word this is one of them. (Sad the way we devalue important words in the search for superlatives.) In the Antarctic I had frequently paused to thank God for letting me live in such a stunning landscape, where scenery and climate produced a stark but sterile world. But where the polar regions have a pure, but severe environment, Machu Picchu added a new kind of majesty; more rounded and prolifically fertile, with peaks crowding together into the far blue distance.

By 1989, when I returned while on a conference trip, it was busy with all the junk that the locals hope to sell to tourists and people were everywhere, walking the Inca trail or doing the geriatric journey by geriatric bus from the railway station.

I loved Peru. The remnants of the pre-Inca stonework are one of the technical wonders of the world and I cannot conceive how people with basic metal and stone tools could carve out massive blocks of stone and fit them together in three dimensions as I might complete a jigsaw puzzle. Go and marvel. I loved the various types of llama/guanaco/alpaca that were everywhere, and I was so fortunate to go back twenty-five years later and wonder at it even more.

### Digression

*On that occasion in 1989 I was at a Scripture Union International conference on the coast and in Lima the capital of Peru. SU had done an amazing work with street children, by which we mean children deserted on the streets to fend for themselves. I heard the stories at first hand of a family whose father died, leaving his mother to marry again, after which 'Jorge', aged seven was taken by car by his step-father to the flea market in Lima and dumped. He survived like every other child like him, by thieving, possibly prostitution and escaping the periodic culls of these kids by the police who, in response to public complaints, allegedly shot them. (This cannot be confirmed but is widely believed.) However, that lay in the future, but was as relevant in 1964 as later.*

*On this second trip to Peru I had the opportunity to spend a bit more time in three places. Lima was a cosmopolitan city, but with miles of suburbs where migrants from the poor mountain areas would look for a better life in the city, where they were caught between Marxist groups who needed them for political pressure, and the police who used what methods they saw fit to control them. Politics in Peru was squalid and violent, and I saw it at first hand.*

*I also had a trip down into Amazonian Peru, to the city of Iquitos, on the river. SU did a good work with street boys there, by teaching a group in the morning and in the afternoon giving them sport and personal support. The aim for most was to help them make a living, at that time, by training them to get and manage a scooter rickshaw taxi.*

*Years later there was a very good initiative by SU and a Scottish team who took a boat across from Scotland (the 'Amazon Hope') which worked up and down the Amazon treating the plagues of eye and other diseases which were endemic. It was a very fruitful experience and I know the Vine Trust continues to increase its number of boats and patients.*

## Ecuador

My contact in Ecuador was a man whose name I forget. He was a doctor who left England to live in a poor community and support with his medical skills the local community and the work of other missionaries. He had spent his adult life learning the local dialect of the Quechua language and eventually translated the Bible into it. He was universally admired for his medical and linguistic skills. I have a picture of him standing astride the Equator. No point in going to the country if you don't have the picture. Those high Andean countries are very volcanic and also poverty-stricken to a greater or less degree. Since my time there they have become associated with political instability, endless drug cultivation, exploitation and poverty.

I met one other American missionary in Ecuador and at the time her name was known in many parts of the world: Marj Saint. Here briefly is her story.

*Operation Auca was an attempt by five Christian missionaries from the United States to bring Christianity to the Waodani or Huaorani people of the rain forest of Ecuador. The Huaorani, also known pejoratively as Aucas, were an isolated tribe known for their violence, against both their own people* and outsiders who entered their territory. With the intention of being the first Christians to evangelise the Huaorani, the missionaries began making regular flights over Huaorani settlements in September 1955, dropping gifts, which were reciprocated. After several months of exchanging gifts, on January 3, 1956, the missionaries established a camp at 'Palm Beach', a sandbar along the Curare river. a few kilometres from Huaorani settlements. Their efforts came to an end on January 8, 1956, when all five – Jim Elliot, Nate Saint, Ed McCully, Peter Fleming and Roger Udarian – were attacked and speared by a group of Huaorani warriors. The news of their deaths was broadcast around the world, and Life magazine covered the event with a photo essay.

Jim Elliot (I think) was the young man who wrote, before going to the Aucas and being well aware of the possible outcome, said, "He is no fool who gives what he cannot keep, to gain what he cannot lose."

How does a woman cope in circumstances like these? Yes, she knew the risks her husband and his friends were taking and accepted that through history people have died for their faith as Jesus warned his followers from the beginning. Nevertheless, the pain is no less when the worst happens. Marj was working with an American Christian broadcaster at the time, while at least two of the bereaved wives went back to the tribe and lived with them, staying long enough to see some embrace the missionaries' faith.

As a missionary kid myself, I knew some of the difficulties all missionaries experience but her sufferings were of a different order entirely. I remember her as a quiet lady with a gentle smile and sad eyes.

## Colombia

Colombia brings to mind a former U.S. soldier who lived anywhere but in the States, so that his limited pension enabled him to live better than he could at home. He was a mine of information about the way to live on $5 a day: cheap sleeping places and shops; transport that cost next to nothing, cafes that spoke English, since the Yanks are even more mono-glot than we are. I benefited from some of his advice in Bogota.

A nice encounter was with a group of young Americans returning home after three years in the Peace Corps. This was an initiative of John Kennedy, the U.S. President at the time, to encourage young people to work with and know their southern neighbours. A young Donald Trump might have been a beneficiary had he been born a bit earlier. He might never have thought of anything so silly as a wall to keep out desperate immigrants from looking for a better living in the USA.

## Panama

Panama had just recovered from some anti-USA riots and I stayed in a cheap hotel beside a burnt out one. Bad town planning had so arranged it that some of the direst slums were separated from the luxury of typical suburban American homes, lawn-encircled and constantly watered, by nothing more than a high wire fence. Each group was an offence to the other.

I have not been back to Latin-America since 1989 when I attended a conference in Peru, but it is disturbing to realise that the population explosion I saw in the twenty-five years between 1964 and 1989 has accelerated since then. Now, thirty years later, the whole area is exploding with drug-fuelled death and destruction, hungry people migrating in their thousands towards Donald Trump's wall. One perceptive friend said, "The Yanks taught us the beauty of capitalism: supply and demand; they demanded coke and we supply it to them." Add to this the various Popes who have forbidden birth control to the poor and the recipe is complete for a poverty-stricken population explosion.

## Costa Rica, Guatemala, Mexico

I had no friends or contacts in the central American republics and no particular memories, but I loved that essential feature of every town or village, the plaza – the square, with a few palm trees and seats for the elderly to sit and watch life passing. In the evening, when the day's work was finished, there was time for young and old to mingle and share the sunset – and a bit of flirting. It gave a sense of community that is often lacking in colder climates.

By this stage I was getting a bit punch drunk and longed for the predictable, ubiquitous, uniformity of American culture and the Peace Corps people were positively slavering for a burger. But first came Mexico. As a boy I had read about Columbus and the Conquistadors, Pizarro and Atahualpa, the invasion of the Spaniards and the insatiable lust for gold, so I was happy to be stunned by the exotic offensiveness of the architecture and the materials of the great buildings. I loved the guitarist who stepped on a bus and sang just for the joie de vivre of it all and left without passing round a hat. I also found myself eating things I otherwise would not have done simply because I hadn't enough Spanish to know better, but I never came to harm. I travelled by bus to the US border and at last I felt at home: coke and burgers and lemon meringue pie and coffee three times a day if possible. I took a bus all the way to El Paso and the border. After that, all sorts of things became possible.

## USA

When I deserted the ship in Montevideo I went to the US embassy for a visa and some dollars. One of the junior staff in the Consulate invited me into his office for coffee because he had never met someone out of Antarctica and anyway, he was bored. I spent a happy hour while he fiddled with my passport and gave me at least one piece of excellent advice. "Buy a Greyhound bus ticket for $99 and you can travel anywhere in the States or Canada for 99 days." I did and it was quite the best advice I ever had. I got on the bus in El Paso and travelled to all sorts of places: Grand Canyon, Phoenix, San Francisco, Los Angeles, and working my way up the west coast spending one night in a cheap hotel and sleeping the next on the bus with breaks for coffee and lemon meringue pie every three hours. My goal was Vancouver after taking the bus up the west coast to the Canadian border. It seems crazy to say so little about the US but I have been to the same places since – and so have many other people (on the box or elsewhere).

One thing in particular sticks in my mind: the spaciousness, the cleanliness, the affluence and, yes, the uniformity of every wayside town or city seemed astonishing after the squashed variety of living in Britain and the endless variety of our regional accents. Of course, a Boston accent is not the same as a Texan or a Dakotan one, but a hamburger is a hamburger and if it is your national dish, it suggests a lack of ambition.

## Canada – again

Vancouver was relatively familiar territory. During my National Service year in Winnipeg training to be a navigator, I had flown from Winnipeg to Victoria for a cricket match but had also had time to make a dash into the Rockies to see an old friend from school days. This time I was carrying greetings and a small gift from a young missionary in Colombia to his parents. In return they treated me royally with a fine dinner in their golf club. From there, the Greyhound bus started through the Rockies and across the prairies. I can't remember anything of great significance until I was back in Winnipeg. My adopted 'family' from RAF days were just as hospitable as before and we were all only five years older. They insisted on getting me an interview on the local TV station. My pictures of the frozen wastes didn't make a great impression: Winnipeg treats temperatures of –40 centigrade and waist-high snow as commonplace. But when I told them that with more than 100,000 free cigarettes available, of the twelve smokers who went down to my base only two came out smoking two years later – this defiance of logic made the evening news.

Then it was on across the prairies again, through the vast Lake of the Woods in Ontario over which I had been horribly lost in the Air Force and ultimately to meeting Jimmy and Joyce in Toronto. I can't remember why they were there rather than Montreal but their abiding memory was my smell. After travelling for so many days without a daily shower Joyce swears that they drove to Montreal with the windows open.

## Homeward

After a while the joys of travelling start to pall. The cheap hotels or the night on the bus, however cheap they may be, make you long for meals at the proper time, hot showers, and home cooking: these fill your consciousness. It was great to remake acquaintances in Montreal but by mutual consent the time soon came for the last couple of legs. The cheapest way across the Atlantic at that time was by Icelandic Airlines from New York, so I got my last pound of flesh from Greyhound, with still about fifty days to spare. Iceland was too good to miss so I lingered long enough to remember that everything smells faintly of sulphur from the thermal volcanic springs that give them central heating. As we left the plane flew over a small island called Surtsey that had appeared from the sea-bed a few months previously. I have a vivid memory of a red-hot centre spewing rocks into the sea in a cloud of steam which reminded me that Iceland is constantly splitting in two – which widens the gap between

Europe and America which is not just geographical but also cultural. We remain friends.

And then we were in Glasgow.

I hadn't said when I would be home but I had phoned from Montreal. I remember walking down Seafield Road in Aberdeen and seeing my Dad walking towards me to buy a newspaper. It was a joyful re-union and I had just enough money left from my two years away to buy my Mum a washing machine. And then it was all over! But what next? Although I had done Sciences and Maths at school and I had done a vacation apprenticeship in Harland and Wolff's Belfast aircraft factory, I concluded that I was not deep-down a scientist or an engineer.

It is probably clear that I come from a family who, to put it mildly, are talkers and there was a certain inevitability about becoming a teacher, so I qualified as such at Aberdeen University and the College of Education.

# Chapter 5  Britain

## Glasgow Academy: 1965 – 69

Throughout Scotland there are Independent Secondary Schools where the children of affluent middle-class citizens get their children educated. In Aberdeen, it was Robert Gordon's College; in Edinburgh, The Academy and Watson's ; in Glasgow it was Glasgow High School and Glasgow Academy. I applied for a job at Glasgow Academy and was appointed. With it went a school flat, which was available to me as a bachelor while looking for a wife.

I started the job with what, looking back, was a wild enthusiasm. Ben Aston, the head of the English department, was on the cusp of retiring after 40 years in the job, fresh from university. The teacher whose job I had taken, had inherited from Ben the traditional Shakespeare play, which I had no intention of doing, in the light of my inexperience. However, there was a memorable morning when Ben and I had a free period and the Staff Room to ourselves. The conversation went something like this.

"Aaah. It is such a pity?"

"What is a pity?"

"Well, there won't be a school play this year. It is forty years since I did Dogberry and Verges sketches from *Much Ado About Nothing* and we have had a show every year since, but now that Peter Gannon has left it is beyond me to do it."

"Ben, don't look at me! This is my first job; there may be an engagement on the horizon somewhere; my flat needs decoration and I couldn't possibly do a play. Moreover, I have decided to do an MEd. at Glasgow University."

"Oh Quite! Quite! You couldn't possibly take it on. All the same, it is such a pity to lose the momentum."

"What about Tony Richards or Andrew Merton?"

"Oh, they have done their stint previously and they are married men with teenage children and they have made it quite clear that it is out of the question."

"That is very understandable, but you take my point that this is not the sort of thing to do in my first year."

"Oh quite! Quite! I do understand. It is just such a pity."

So, of course, I eventually agreed on condition that John Horrex would do the staging if I got the words into the players. There was a play – *The Merchant of Venice*; there were volunteers and auditions and the makings of a caste, which created a huge row, or more specifically a Shylock row. The first I knew of it, I was violently accosted by the Deputy Head.

"Don't you dare take AJ to be Shylock! He is doing a scholarship for Cambridge this year and he can't afford a minute to do a major part in the play."

"Sorry: I didn't know, but he is very able and also very good."

"Well keep your hands off him."

And then a wonderful sequel when the boy's parents asked to see me during the following lunch time.

"Thank you so much for putting on the school play. We would love Andrew to play Shylock and we have told Mr Varley that if he can't do the scholarship and the play he doesn't deserve the scholarship."

"You have actually told Mr Varley this?" I asked.

"Yes. He wasn't pleased."

I did two more plays: *Richard the Second* and *The Royal Hunt of the Sun* by Peter Schaeffer. The first of these was designed as a farewell to Ben Aston, my old Head of Department. He had started the tradition so I was looking for a play with a part for Ben and the perfect choice was *Richard the Second*. In it there is a famous speech in which the Old Duke sees the mess the young King Richard is making of the country, beginning with

> Methinks I am a prophet new inspired,
>  and thus expiring do foretell of him,
>  this fierce, wild blaze or riot cannot last
> for violent fires soon burn out themselves;
>  small showers last long, but sudden showers are short . . .

and he goes on to predict a disastrous end to the riotous excesses of the King. The speech ends with a glorious eulogy about the wonders of England,

> This royal throne of kings, this sceptered isle,
> this earth of majesty, this seat of Mars,
> this other Eden, demi-paradise,
> this fortress built by Nature for herself
> against infection and the hand of war,
> this blessed plot, this earth, this realm,

this England . . .
   is now leased out, like to a tenement
or pelting farm, I die pronouncing it . . .
that England that was wont to conquer others
has made a shameful conquest of herself . . .

The point was that every day Ben would fulminate in a similar way about the decline of Britain under a Labour Government as he stood, back to the fire, *Times* in hand, describing the national disasters that lay ahead. He got huge applause.

*Many years later I was at a meeting in the Glasgow offices of the BBC which were a stone's throw from Ben's home. So I made a visit, not knowing if he was still alive. He was, and his wife invited me in. Ben was bed-ridden but very much alive.*

*"Ah, young Kimber! Come in; sit down. I hear you are a refugee from the classroom."*

*I asked how he passed his time and he called for his wife to bring a cardboard shoe box. It contained a number of cassette recording tapes which contained all the poems he knew by heart, including Matthew Arnold's 'Sorab and Rustum' which is almost a thousand lines long. There were many hours of recorded poetry.*

*It was a privilege to know him.*

*The Royal Hunt of the Sun* was a very dramatic departure from Shakespeare and I did it because of my South American journeys. It deals with the Spanish conquest of Peru and the scandalous way the Conquistadors conquered and enslaved the Inca tribes in pursuit of gold. However, we were halfway through rehearsals when someone said, "I assume you have permission from the Performing Rights Society", of whom I had never heard. I wrote to them in a sweat of anxiety and the first line of the reply made it worse.

"The play is released only for professional performance." Panic! "However, in the circumstances since you are an amateur, school performance. You may go ahead."

I involved three friends who lectured in the Royal Scottish Academy of Music and Drama and they produced some terrifying music and dance for the scene in which the Inca and his followers were massacred in Cuzco.

Occasionally one meets former pupils in later life, and one pupil did cross my path many years later. In those days corporal punishment was an accepted (if rare) resort if appropriate, and the belt was the usual implement. The pupil in question was an inveterate talker when silence was required. When threats failed, I would send a pupil to get the strap from a master who kept such a device if required and by the time the pupil had gone to get the strap he was usually sufficiently subdued to make the use of the implement unnecessary. On this one occasion all my verbal comments had not stopped the stream of gossip, so I sent the culprit to get the belt and on this one occasion I actually used it.

Our paths crossed many years later when he was the Moderator of the General Assembly of the Church of Scotland.

## The Cadet Force

The next thing I rushed into was the Cadet Force. Glasgow Academy was developed as a memorial to former pupils who died in the Great War, so a cadet force was an essential part of the school. I don't think there was an RAF section at the time but it didn't matter since the basic activities of marching up and down were common to all. The crunch came in the holidays and particularly the Easter holidays on Arran when the senior boys would bivouac in two-man tents and the juniors would sleep in the annex to the Lochranza hotel. My three years included weather so hot that one boy collapsed with heat-stroke; on the second, we were washed out of our tents and had to cut short our climb so that we could sleep in the hotel – which caught fire when wet clothes broke the rope of a pulley so that anoraks started to burn on the hot plate. In the third year the weather was so bad that all seventy of us slept overnight in the Territorial Army buildings.

These are character-forming experiences.

## Meeting Hilda

At much the same time as this was starting, I was invited to dinner with a family who had connections to my sister in Aberdeen. Murray and Dorothy Collins lived in a quarter of one of those vast Victorian mansions just off the Great Western Road in Kelvinside. They had three children of school age – Jane, Sasha and Bart. Dorothy was very generous in her invitations to a bachelor living normally on two boiled eggs each evening after a long day at school and at the University. This, however, was dinner, with other guests, just one of whom was Hilda Caldwell, and her parents John and Ruby. It was a put-up job, of course. Hilda had the same Christian background as I had and she was in every way suitable, particularly in that we were both single – and getting on. I was 29 and Hilda 23. It was a fix, but looking back over our 50+ years of marriage, it was a perfect fulfilment for each of us. By general consent in my family, I needed to settle down and be an honest citizen, which implied the need for someone to settle me down.

Our first date was, of all things, to Wagner's opera, *The Valkyries*. That may have been a bit of swank on my part, but anyone who sits through some very tough – and long – music has endured a test of some kind and all that followed showed that Hilda loved music and had stamina.

Dorothy, not to mention Hilda's parents, had a twinge of anxiety, as it seemed we might hit it off. After all, I was obviously a restless soul and if you earn your living in life insurance, you don't want to invest your daughter in an unstable partnership. I invited Hilda and parents to a meal in my bachelor school flat, which was well placed on the border between Kelvinside (posh) and Maryhill (not posh at all). To be brief, one day we went to Largs and I tentatively raised the question of marriage: not a straight proposal; but more of a "what do you think about possibly getting engaged?" The omens were not good, because Hilda had one of those lingering ailments beginning with a 'd' which takes away the appetite. On the whole we thought it was a possibility and eventually an engagement was announced, but at one stage when presents were being received and plans were under way, she was sure that she would have to give them all back: but she didn't and 50+ years later we are very glad.

Our loving children describe our engagement as two elderly, desperate people clinging together.

Hilda's parents were full of trepidation but kept it fairly well under control by briskly deciding that a rented flat in Kelvinside/Maryhill was not a good long-term prospect so we were guided into buying a small, new terrace house in Bearsden (posh) and a twenty-five-year mortgage, which put a pretty emphatic seal on the whole business. Suddenly, I was no longer a free agent but a citizen with growing responsibilities. We got a car in place of the mini-van which was suitable for a mere bachelor but emphatically not for Father Caldwell's daughter. Thus, I was enabled to go to school and Hilda to a new job with the Glasgow and West of Scotland College of Domestic Science, where she would lecture in Dress and Design. It was a great arrangement since the two workplaces were less than half a mile apart and, in addition, both were half a mile from the University where I eventually completed my MEd.

We began married life in a new terraced house in a small development near a golf course. Had we been more knowledgeable about houses we might have paused to wonder why there was an empty house across the road which looked new, but dilapidated, and was used by the builders for their tea breaks – but we didn't. We later discovered that there was settlement, not only in the tea-break house but in ours. The four houses in our block were built on a concrete raft supported on piles driven into the ground, but the steps at the back and the porch at the front were not. They eventually sank away from the house. The builder made no reply to complaints from any of the householders.

So I wrote to the Glasgow evening paper which was published on Friday. My long lie-in on Saturday was interrupted by a ring at the door.

"Good morning. I am from the *Evening Express*. Tell me about the settlement across the road . . . "

Shortly after the bell rang again: "Good morning. I am from BBC Scotland . . ."

On Monday morning the builder started to demolish the house across the road, having previously ignored all our requests for action.

One reason for the move was that I had done four years at the Academy and felt I had made enough mistakes and had also learned the appropriate lessons. Despite many reasons to stay put, there were several to move on, and particularly, one major event and that was the death of our first baby.

Hilda went into labour and I took her to hospital. I can see and hear everything that happened with perfect clarity. An embarrassed doctor came to the waiting room and said, "I am afraid the baby has died. He just drew one breath and could not be resuscitated, so it was not a still birth."

It was a strange experience in that initially neither Hilda nor I had a great sense of grief as would be expected. Even more than that Hilda had a perfect calmness through the visits from family and friends that astonished everyone, including herself.

However, there followed a reaction when each of us separately had a great outrush of grief over this lost little life and the emptiness that follows nine months of eager expectation.

With Father Caldwell we had a very simple little interment at the cemetery: a couple of prayers of thankfulness and commitment to God for the small life and the need to adjust and go on.

## Glasgow University: MEd

The 'going on' included the completion of my MEd. Glasgow Academy was only half a mile from Glasgow University. Having done my teacher training at Aberdeen University and the College of Education, I investigated the possibility of doing a Masters in Education and found that this could be done over three years externally, with one year on Education, one year on Educational Psychology and the third year on a thesis.

I have a sense of guilt about the course, because I should have done so much more work for it, but obviously all the events mentioned above gave little time for serious reading, particularly on educational psychology, beyond borrowing Murray and Dorothy's children to do intelligence tests for practice. Looking back on those events, the tests were in a limited sense a guide to later school performance, but not a great predictor of life performance.

My thesis was 'A study of the use of the word "Nature" in the educational thought of Rousseau, Calvin and Comenius.' No publisher offered me a contract.

## Glasgow to Southport (1969 – 73)

I then applied for and got a job as Deputy Headmaster at a Christian secondary school in Southport . Lancashire. It was to be an eventful four years in many ways. For a start, there was the house. The town of Southport was built on sand which stretched from the Lancashire plane across to Blackpool, a distance so long and a slope so gradual that I never saw the tide fully in at Southport. Allegedly it did but I never saw it and we certainly reaped the consequences.

We looked at a fine detached house with front and rear gardens whose owners were the parents of the man who made model animals for Ken Dodd, the comedian: that is distinction for you. The other feature of the house was the settlement, which, in turn, was caused by the sandy soil. ("The wise man built his house upon the rock but the foolish one . . .")

We bought it and moved in but when we saw the very obvious slant that would take a dropped tennis ball straight across the front room from door to window in a couple of seconds. We phoned the friendly architect who had encouraged us to buy and said we couldn't possibly live in it, he said, "But every house in Southport has settlement problems: just live with it."

Instead, we borrowed £1,000 from the building society which paid for a builder to knock down the entire front of the house and half the side wall and then build it up again – as good as new, nearly. When we moved four years later it sold for £11,000. But there was always the evidence of settlement and when we eventually moved there was a real sense of relief and a determination to live in straight houses in future.

## Southport – The Boys

We had four interesting years in Southport, without ever feeling it was home, but it was home to Ashley and Barry, born in the local hospital. Both births were closely supervised by a lovely matron and friend who was determined, in the light of our first baby's death, that all would go well – and it did. Ashley's birth was close in time to that of my nephew Jeremy Craig, and we have a photo of the two of them at opposite ends of a splendid pram. The pram, by today's standards, was more of a chariot, with elaborate springs to minimise the effect of bumps in the pavement.

Barry's arrival was more of a surprise. Hilda began labour one evening and I took her into hospital, leaving me with the sole care of a sleeping infant. Next morning, I was trying to feed, and clothe the youthful Ash and then deliver him to a friend while I went off to earn a living. The phone rang while I was adjusting a nappy and I was inclined to swear but didn't, wondering who would ring at such an inopportune moment. The answer was Hilda announcing the arrival of Barry. So glad I didn't swear.

## Southport – The School

Scarisbrick Hall School was the creation of an interesting man, called Charles Oxley, who was determined to run a school on Christian principles, which included morning prayers for all pupils and clear discipline. It provided time for a hymn, a very short Bible-based comment and a prayer. Uniforms were obligatory. Pupils were a mixed bag from absolutely brilliant to many who had failed the eleven plus exam which gave entry to state secondary schools, and we had a record of producing good results for many.

I had four years there as Deputy Head, but eventually moved on. I had a great admiration for Charles Oxley. Any man who infiltrates a paedophile ring in order to provide the evidence to send them to jail, deserves great admiration. The down side of having firm convictions is that you expect others to share them. To a great extent I did, but I also had to intervene to prevent some pupils from being arbitrarily expelled. Having had five years at a Public School run on Christian lines, I found the Scarisbrick model rather

66

old-fashioned and out of step with changes in wider society. But we did a number of new things. I ran ski holidays to Austria and Aviemore which were very worthwhile, but one holiday was life-changing in many ways.

## The Scott Boys

The school had a small boarding department which included pupils whose parents were missionaries. Two of these boys were Andrew and Alistair Scott. Towards the end of the summer term of our first year, before we had our first baby, Ashley, we discovered that their guardians, an elderly couple living in Northern Ireland, were unable to take them for the holidays, so we agreed that they would come and stay with us. In many ways it was a life-changing decision with long-term consequences.

For a start, they bickered and occasionally fought. On at least one occasion a chess set in use was sent flying across the room when the losing person got rather cross. The trouble was that they were very different in ways that jarred on each other. One was taciturn, the other loquacious; the younger resented authority and the older liked to assert it: there were always combustible opportunities and they rather liked to take them. They came with us to Scotland, which included driving over the border where Drew spat on England as we left and Alistair spat on Scotland as we arrived, for reasons which I have never discovered or understood. Then we landed on my sister Carol and husband Stephen Cordiner at Lynnwood, in Aberdeen, that home from home for the scattered Kimber family. From there we went down the interminable road to Campbeltown, stopping to camp at the side of loch Fyne.

Hilda's sister Marion had married Bob Craig and they lived in Campbeltown, which is a town no-one visits by accident. It is at the end of the long Argyll Peninsula and about one hundred and forty miles from Glasgow. When you get there, it is well worth the trouble for its beauty and its surroundings, not least the view across to Ireland from the end of the peninsula. Bob was a native, an accountant, a pillar of his local church and the wider community. They were immensely hospitable to visiting sailors and anyone associated with the Royal Naval Reserve. Bob had been a navigator in the Fleet Air Arm during National Service and continued the connection in the Royal Naval Reserve. Their hospitality extended to the Kimbers and their temporary charges and we were royally entertained. Bob and Marion, as always, were very generous with their hospitality – and probably also with

Bob's boat. Both sets of relatives gave us what the boys said was the best holiday they had ever had, and Hilda and I were very grateful.

We then took the boys to the home of my married sister, Carol, and her husband Stephen Cordiner. Stephen was a wonderfully generous and hospitable brother-in-law to me and indeed to all our family over many years. They lived in Bieldside, a suburban village on Deeside about five miles from Aberdeen city. Stephen and his family were from a Brethren background, so a brief summary will explain what that meant.

## The Brethren Churches

*Maybe this is the place to explain about the Brethren movement which played such a formative influence in our lives. First a brief historical background.*

*The Christian church has always been developing fresh responses to changes in culture and society, both within and outside existing denominations. In the 1830s a number of people were looking for changes to the existing denominational patterns of worship, at least one of which looked for a return to the simplicity of the early church in New Testament times. This involved a close reading of the New Testament in relation to early Victorian society.*

*A few remarkable men, including George Muller and others of his generation, took the view that the simplicity of church order in the book of Acts was just as applicable in Victorian society. The phrase 'in simple dependence on God' characterised the way Muller lived, particularly in the orphanage he set up. In a time of cholera, he found orphaned children coming to him for help and, as he said, he had no resources except prayer, and he found his prayers being answered in surprising ways. He made it a principle to solicit gifts from no-one but God and found his needs constantly being supplied. Other men were looking for a kind of worship that reflected the simple, unplanned model of New Testament practice. The Brethren rejected ecclesiastical structures and each 'assembly' was autonomous, although there were close relations with like-minded groups. It was a very closely linked yet autonomous structure and their missionary zeal was extraordinary.*

*At the time of writing they have sent more than 5,600 missionaries abroad.*

*These were ideas for their time and were a contrast to the formality of the established church and existing denominations.. My parents were missionaries who practised these principles of living 'in dependence on God'. We will see how these principles worked out in practice.*

## Southport to Balerno

After four years – and two children – in Southport we came to the conclusion that Scarisbrick Hall was not a long-term job for me. I knew that Mr Oxley, the Headmaster, was looking for a long-term appointment but we had enough disagreements to suggest that I was not the one. I found Scarisbrick was too much of a one-man band, so I got a job at Stevenson College, in Edinburgh and we bought a house in Dalmahoy Crescent, Balerno, having got a surprisingly good price for our repaired settlement house in Southport. The Balerno house was detached with a decent bit of garden at front and back. People like us lived in the surrounding homes and there were children of Ash and Barry's age. After a bit of church-hunting we settled happily in St Mungo's Episcopal Church, which was essentially Anglican, and we were happy members there for all the boys' school days.

My job was in the English Department of Stevenson College of Further Education, a few miles from Balerno. It was a refreshing change from secondary school, with a range of students from plumbers and joiners to international students wanting to improve their English and get good Highers. Several members of staff lived in Balerno and car sharing made for easy travel.

Highlights of the Balerno days need a chapter of their own, but one major one was that Hilda's mother was in poor health and it was likely that she would need care. Moving to Campbeltown and the care of Hilda's sister, Marion, was not an option, so it was agreed that we would find a bigger house in Balerno. We moved to 438 Lanark Rd West, on the main road into Edinburgh and Mum and Dad Caldwell came to stay. By that time Mum had had two strokes and had difficulty speaking, which was a sore trial to a vigorous conversationalist. Shortly after the move, she died at home. Dad stayed and later built an extension onto the house with a large bed and sitting room with bathroom and kitchen. It was a happy arrangement until he later married Lena Rossiter and moved away for a time, When Lena died he moved back to us.

## The Scottish Examination Board (1975 – 96)

In my second year at Stevenson College my Head of Department came into my room and said, "Here is a job that might interest you," and it did.

"The Scottish Examination Board is looking for an Examination Officer with suitable qualifications to service Subject Panels in Arts subjects . . ."

I applied and was interviewed, in a smallish building at Causewayside in Edinburgh, by the Director, Dr Urquhart and the Depute Director, Dr John Walker. Dr Urquhart was about to retire so, if appointed, Dr Walker would be my boss. I must have mentioned that I was working on a book in a series for SU looking at Christian beliefs for secondary school children. They asked if school age children were interested in such things and I said, "Well my book is about the World, the Flesh and the Devil," and they know enough about those things to make it worthwhile." I got the job, and very interesting it turned out to be.

There were other Examination Officers and among us we covered all the subjects examined, so my share was English, History, Geography, Modern Studies, Business Studies, Economics and Music. My friend Hamish covered the Sciences and another, Jim, did the Maths and the statistics, which was a large part of the Board's business.

It was an interesting time to be at the Board because the Government was at last raising the school-leaving age to sixteen so both curriculum and examinations would have to be totally revised to cover the entire ability range. Prior to that pupils could leave at fifteen without any formal assessment, so it was a crucial time for the whole system.

For every subject there was a Panel of specialists who were responsible for supervising both the curriculum and the exams that would assess what pupils had learnt by the time they left school. Each Panel would have a couple of teachers, a college of education lecturer, an HM Inspector and someone from a University. An exchange of views at my first Panel meeting, which was Music, gave an insight into the sort of issues which would arise. The University representative turned out to be the Professor of Music (and, by coincidence, the father of a pupil of mine at Glasgow Academy who, to the great surprise of his family, performed in the school play).

His contribution to the Panel immediately identified the difference in the new task before the Board. The Prof. said, "Well I hope we can set really high standards in keyboard skills for more, well-prepared, students at the University." There was an immediate, angry response from a headteacher from Huntly who said, "That is not the task of this panel. We are here to develop a meaningful and honest curriculum for every pupil who wants to develop his musical ability for any and every musical instrument."

So, there would be musical instruments and musical experience in line with what pupils actually listened to and performed on, as opposed to, but including, an elitist university-driven course.

The main problem was finding a way to assess both the most and the least competent students in each subject and the final arrangement was to have tests in each subject at three levels, called Credit, General and Foundation, with the advice that each student could attempt two adjacent levels, namely Credit and General or General and Foundation. So there would be the possibility of tackling a test that would be attainable but would also challenge. That in a nutshell, was the change the Government was wanting to effect.

## New Examinations

It was a great time to be in the exam business. At the centre of the development were two Publications chaired by Head Teachers with a high profile in the Scottish Educational World, Messrs Munn and Dunning; the first covering curriculum and the other assessment. It meant that in every subject of the secondary curriculum there would be a Subject Panel with the usual representation of Secondary, Higher and Technical Education. Throughout Scottish Education there was endless discussion about what it meant for individual people, and more immediately, what would it mean for us in the Exam Board.

To be brief, a number of our senior colleagues decided they didn't want the hassle of ten years' stress and upheaval so they took early retirement. First, John Walker, the Director took early retirement, and Melvin Hendry, the Depute Director, chose to play golf and avoid an early grave. Then Jim Milne, the Senior Exam Officer decided that fishing on the Tweed was a better chance for a long life than bringing a new system to birth. Quite suddenly Hamish Long was the Director and I was the Depute with responsibility for developing the new exam system.

## Dyslexia and Physical Disabilities

There are people who have difficulty spelling the occasional word and there are others who find it hard to spell a single word correctly and a whole range of difficulty between these extremes. This had been a particular problem for public examinations. Should poor spelling be ignored in all subjects except English? Was bad spelling a medical condition and if so which branch of medicine should fix it?

But the more it was discussed the more difficult it seemed to be. Chemistry teachers pointed out that spelling was very important in the laboratory. The difference between a sulphite and a sulphate could be very serious. It was also a distressing problem for parents whose children were afflicted. One senior civil servant on our committee was asked what parents of a dyslexic child felt and he said one word: "Anguish."

It was decided that the time had come to address the problem once and for all. Apparently, it was my job to do it, and very interesting it was. In the first place, was this a neurological condition, and should doctors fix it? Absolutely not, was the general response; it is a psychological issue for the educational psychologists, so we invited all the Scottish professionals to gather at the Board. I selected ten scripts from the current English exam which showed varying degrees of bad spelling from, trivial to almost illegible and invited them to divide the simply careless spellers from those who had a clear disorder.

The next stage was for subject specialists to decide how important it was in their subject and what penalties, if any, should be applied. Was there a definable point where bad spelling became a disability rather than carelessness?

This broadened out into the wider question of physical disability and how this could be addressed when all sixteen-year-olds were being examined for the first time, including young people who previously had left school at age fifteen. Suffice it to say that one specialist in the dyslexia field, was kind enough to say that we were "light years ahead of other countries and exam boards".

However, all the British exam boards eventually worked out common ways to address the spelling problem, by offering extra time or, in extreme cases, a scribe to whom a candidate could dictate answers, on the grounds that we were assessing subject knowledge rather than presentation. Each subject panel prescribed its own approach.

At the same time the Exam Board assumed responsibility from Her Majesty's Inspectors of School for assessing all kinds of disabilities. I was urged to spend time and travel to see as many candidates as possible and this was a very humbling task. I developed a huge respect for loving parents and dedicated teachers in special schools.

# Chapter 6 The World

## The Seychelles

While these developments were being discussed, I was working in the office I shared with my colleague Hamish Long, when John Walker, the director at that time, came in. His first words to me were, "How would you like three weeks in the Seychelles?" Stunned silence from me and silent outrage from Hamish. The background to the question was that a friend of our Director had been on holiday in those exotic islands, and had discussed with the local Director of Education, some of the political problems she faced with a very left-wing Government. She thought a report from a detached observer might help her.

To my great surprise, I soon found myself on a plane to Nairobi en route to Victoria, the capital of the Seychelles. The final approach takes the plane between, and uncomfortably close to two great black rocky peaks as we descended to the airport. I was met by Madame d'Ofay, the head of the Education Department and was taken to a homely hotel surrounded by grounds filled with exotic vegetation. Mangos seemed to be constantly available which is every child's dream. I ate my first guinea pig – unwittingly, which is the best way. My modest hotel had a pile of left-behind books from generations of tourists, which was just as well as it happened.

Everything that can be said about tropical paradises applies to the Seychelles, so we take that as given, but real life goes on there in much the same way as everywhere else. The economy is dependent on basic agriculture plus whatever tourism can bring and that depends on politics, which, at the time of my visit were very tense.

A coup d'état had put in power a left-wing government while the President had been at a conference in London. There was active support from Russia and other socialist powers, since the islands are in a strategic position in the Indian ocean. When I asked the local teachers what a true socialist curriculum would be like they stressed that it should emerge from the material and social world the kids lived in. For example, they wanted kids to understand how houses were made from local materials, so the chemistry of coral was discovered by heating it to make quick lime and thence cement, and the learning process would end with some brick-laying and a political element about the dignity of labour and the nature of a socialist society. This was going to be a long and interesting process.

In fact, everything changed overnight. I was vaguely aware of distant shooting one afternoon, but I paid no attention to it. The next morning, I was woken by my landlady who said that a group of South African mercenaries had attempted a coup d'état. The full story gradually emerged. The group had flown in from Angola, which at that time was in a state of constant conflict. They came bearing gifts for the local children and ostensibly coming to play rugby with local teams. *"Timeo Danaos et dona ferentes"* – "I fear Greeks bearing gifts."

Once through customs, they planned to storm the government buildings, taking as hostages the Cabinet and then invite the ousted Prime Minster to return from London. Only the vigilance of a customs officer saved the situation by asking for one box of 'presents' to be opened, revealing a machine gun and live rounds of ammunition. Immediately the disguise was discarded and the mercenaries seized the airport and the control tower. The next plane to arrive was an Air India one bound for South Africa so they commandeered it, and most of the mercenaries got on board, leaving a small unfortunate group to do the best they could by escaping into the mountains.

From my point of view all I could do was obey the curfew and stay in the hotel until the mercenaries had all been found. Fortunately, generations of guests had left their reading matter behind – but there was no TV. What was happening in the world outside our small islands? A week later most of the fugitive mercenaries had been captured, but there were thought to be others in the jungle. However, the curfew was lifted and I was able at last to go for a walk into the town – until a car screeched to a halt beside me. A policeman and a large Tanzanian soldier got out and accosted me.

"You are one of the mercenaries: get into the car."

"I assure you I am not: if you ask Madame d'Ofay at the Ministry of Education . . ."

"Get into the car."

It is a great comfort to be innocent and able to prove it, but I would not have liked to be one of the guilty party. I had a lengthy wait in the police HQ and became aware that the door was slightly ajar and a strange man was watching me, presumably checking my appearance against a mug shot of the guilty. I was released but there was little appetite for much more research, on my part or that of the Ministry. I made and presented my report, recommending, for the sake of potential leaders of the country, that they should have a curriculum that would enable their ablest young people to find further and higher education abroad. The Cabinet received it with their thanks and I was given an enormous 'coco-de-mer' as a token of their esteem. I knew it was rare and highly valued as an aphrodisiac. Madame d'Ofay treated me to an interesting lunch of octopus and local vegetables and we parted with mutual respect. I flew out and headed for home – only to find that the coco-de-mer and its aphrodisiac properties had been stolen en route.

Back home I found that the weather had been exceptionally cold and indeed, the reservoir at Balerno was frozen with a very thick layer of ice. Hilda had first heard of the Seychelles coup d'état through an early morning phone call from a former pupil of mine at the BBC news desk.

"Is Peter all right?" he asked.

"Why would he not be?"

"Have you not heard? There is a coup d'etat in the Seychelles".

" I am sure he will be OK," she said.

And I was.

## Cairo

I gradually realised that there is a small industry of consultants who seem to travel the globe disbursing wisdom. Because they are brought in at some expense to the tax-payer they are called 'experts' when they arrive. I was first called an expert in Egypt, and although I protested that I was just someone who worked in the exam business, the name somehow stuck. My invitation came by a genuine expert who worked in educational research and to spare his blushes I will call him Richard. He rang the Exam Board, where I worked and asked if I could be free to come with him to Cairo, since he had a contract to advise the Egyptian government about exams and had no examination experience. My boss kindly released me to fly out to Cairo, but I must say I went with some misgivings. Richard had booked me in to a hotel near the ministry and we had a congenial meal together. I like to think that we made a good team.

The 'Thanawiya Amma' had for many years been the model for public exams throughout the Middle East, developed in Egypt and copied with minor variation in many other Middle-Eastern countries. The Egyptian Government felt a change was needed. The exams were set by the national Inspectors of schools, much as had been the case in Scotland before the Exam Board was established. My first recommendation was that they needed a separate body, as was the case in Europe. This would liberate Inspectors of schools to concentrate on their main job of developing teachers and maintaining standards.

Then came the suggestion that the Americans would also like to make a contribution, which meant a separate visit to Cairo for me and a meeting with Woody, a charming linguist from Princeton University. Joint projects between Yanks and Brits had a poor reputation, but we got on famously. At the end of the first visit I suddenly remembered that I had not bought a present for my wife and nor had Woody. Time was short and we both settled for a handbag bought from the gift shop in the hotel.

We came back for a second visit a month later.

"How did the handbag go down?" I asked.

Woody winced.

"Well," he said, "I have a sister with very bad taste in matters of clothes and accessories, and my wife just said, 'I think you should give the bag to your sister.' What about you?"

"I am not too sure. I just know that I haven't seen the bag since I bought it and I have the feeling it will stay that way."

When away on working trips I try to find a church that offers a service in English, and Cairo had an Anglican cathedral not far from my hotel. It shared a large site with an English Language private school and I was introduced to the Headmaster whose face was vaguely familiar. Lying in bed I suddenly remembered the connection. A good friend of mine was at one time the Chaplain of a well-known independent school in Scotland, and he got on badly with the Head Teacher, to the point where my friend said to me, "You know, the relationship was so difficult I had to ask God to remove the Head Teacher – and do you know, God sent him to Egypt."

In Cairo there was an Anglican cathedral which I attended when possible. It was in the same compound as an English-speaking High School and on one occasion the Headmaster was at a service. I had that vague feeling that we had met before somewhere – and we had – in an Edinburgh school.

The Egyptian work continued and the Government agreed to the establishment of a separate Examination body along the lines of our recommendations. Two senior women officials from the new body came to Scotland to see our operation and they came around the beginning of May. They were absolutely ecstatic when we met. "Your country is the most beautiful in the world. It is a mosaic of yellow and green. We have never seen anything so beautiful." And indeed, to see a landscape with alternating fields of yellow oilseed and new wheat is a delight to the eyes, especially if you take-off from the Egyptian desert, then land in Scottish spring time.

*A side trip up the Nile. During a national holiday I flew up the Nile to Luxor and took in a 'son et Lumiere' presentation at night, which gave a splendidly dramatic look at the procession of Pharaohs who had outbid each other in the size and magnificence of their public and religious buildings, but most of all in their tombs. Interesting as it certainly was the words of Shelley's poem 'Ozymandias' were never far from my mind.*

I met a traveller from an antique land,
who said – "Two vast and trunkless legs of stone
stand in the desert. . . . Near them, on the sand,
half sunk a shattered visage lies, whose frown,
and wrinkled lip, and sneer of cold command,
tell that its sculptor well those passions read
which yet survive, stamped on these lifeless things,
the hand that mocked them, and the heart that fed;
and on the pedestal, these words appear:
My name is Ozymandias, King of Kings;
Look on my Works, ye Mighty, and despair!
Nothing beside remains. Round the decay
of that colossal Wreck, boundless and bare
the lone and level sands stretch far away."

*(Shelley's Poetry and Prose, 1977 - Poetry Foundation online)*

It is a good poem reminding humanity that '*sic transit gloria mundi*'; human pride leaves monuments which simply ridicule our own vanity with the reminder that we too shall be mocked in due course. Nevertheless, we still don't understand the extraordinary precision of the pyramids' dimensions, nor how they structured and built them with their precise orientation to the stars – and much else. Mighty works indeed!

On a second visit to Egypt I had a more satisfying journey into the desert with my colleague Richard. In the third and fourth centuries C.E. the Christian churches in Egypt developed a new approach to spirituality by a man who acquired the name of St Anthony. Finding the business and noise of city life a distraction from 'the pursuit of God' he retired into a remote part of the desert where he found a cave to live in and a spring of water, sufficient to meet his needs and the cultivation of enough food to live on.

*Here is a summary of his life and work:*

*The best known 'Desert Father' was Anthony the Great, who moved to the desert in AD 270–271 and became known as both the father and founder of desert monasticism. By the time Anthony had died in AD 356, thousands of monks and nuns had been drawn to living in the desert following Anthony's example, leading his biographer, Athanasius of Alexandria, to write that "the desert had become a city".–The Desert Fathers had a major influence on the development of Christianity.*

(St Anthony of Egypt, Lion Dictionary of Quotations, page 20)

The site of Antony's settlement has been in continuous use ever since and I went there twice. It is now surrounded by a high wall with a strong gate, a development necessitated by periodic attacks from enemies of several kinds. Outside the gates there is accommodation for visitors who may stay as long as they wish. Inside the gates there is an oasis with space to grow palm trees and vegetables which at times have been life-saving. The monks are gracious to visitors and food and water are always offered. The site has been occupied continuously since the third century.

The impulse that drove Anthony into the desert continues and there is a saying that when the monasteries thrive, so does the church and the converse is true. Best of all I like the instructions for disposal of his property after death: "Let Bishop Athanasius have the sheepskin I sleep on, which he gave me new and which has grown old with me. As for my hairshirt, keep it for yourself."

I am bound to say that St Anthony's retreat was more congenial than the Cathedral in Cairo.

## Estonia

When Communism collapsed and the Berlin wall fell in1988 we got a call from the British Council asking if someone from Estonia could visit the Exam Board on a fact-finding visit. There was great political confusion in the Baltic Republics, which had been in the Soviet bloc, but Estonians were trying to find a way into greater political freedom and independence. Erik was a teacher who had received funding from the British Council to see what was happening in the UK, and Scotland, with its own system of education, was a more natural partner in size than England with its several examination boards. We gave Erik a warm welcome, the more so as we understood what it meant to be a small part of a larger economic and social union. Estonians were a fiercely independent country with their own language and particularly its own musical culture. After visiting a number of schools and seeing our assessment arrangements, it was agreed that I would pay a short visit to Tallin, the capital.

Historically Estonia and its neighbours Latvia and Lithuania had always been caught between Russia and Germany while retaining their cultural identities and in Estonia folk songs were central. I was shown a natural amphitheatre outside Tallin where for many years an annual singing festival was held and its continuation through the communist years, was crucial to their survival as a country. At the time of my visit there was a lot of tension about the Russian population, which amounted to about forty percent, and some Russians were beginning to move over the border but with no guarantee that this would continue.

Then on August 23rd 1989 about two million Estonians, Latvians and Lithuanians joined hands in a 690-kilometer human chain across the three Baltic countries in protest at Soviet occupation. It was a very moving sight and the most emphatic political statement. Later all three countries joined NATO.

## Relations with other Examination Boards and Countries

Scotland has always been proud of its own educational system and indeed we were the first country to establish examinations for university entrance with the Highers in 1888. However, it was in the interests of all concerned that we should have regular meetings with the examination boards in England, Wales and Northern Ireland. I particularly remember when the Northern Ireland Board were hosts and the meetings were held in Queen's University just a few hundred yards from my Grandmother's house. It was a time when 'the troubles' were at their worst and the Principal of the University thanked us warmly for coming. He made the point that so many of their most promising young people were choosing to "cross the water", as he put it, to the rest of Britain for university. Arising from that meeting we had further contact with Northern Ireland when Mrs Thatcher decreed that there should be national testing for primary schools in Maths and English. While preparations were in hand, we had a fraternal visit from our colleagues in Northern Ireland who were beginning to make their own plans and at some stage we floated the idea that we should include Northern Ireland in the process. The population of Northern Ireland was under two million, while Scotland's was five and half million, so it was agreed that we would develop material for both Boards and this proved to be beneficial for both sides. We made a modest income from it.

## The International Association for Educational Assessment

The Scottish Examination Board, for whom I worked was affiliated to a network of people working in the same trade in other countries and it was a part of my job to attend annual meetings, which were hosted by different countries in turn. Delegates attending these conferences sometimes carried bags with the initials of this body on their brief cases, in the hopes that fellow-travellers would assume that we were going to the International Atomic Energy Authority rather than to an organisation for making life hard for teenagers.

My first trip was to Des Moines, the State capital of Iowa in the USA, a state I think I once visited while in the RAF during a holiday from Winnipeg. Both places qualify for the flattest places on earth with Winnipeg probably just pushing it into second place. The great plain which runs down the centre of north America is unmatched for the vast space dedicated to feeding the hungry with cereals, which runs from Hudson Bay to the Gulf of Mexico and it is from the swamps of Manitoba and Iowa that the Mississippi starts its majestic journey through the heart of America.

To be fair, what Iowa lacks in scenic attraction it compensates with the warmth of its hospitality. Unhappily I was seduced at dinner time by a help-yourself buffet featuring roast beef as only the Americans can do it, but as a mere Brit I didn't understand why the label above the food said, "Surf and Turf"; but within the hour my allergy to all kinds of shell fish made me very unwell. However, my discomfort was matched by a charming event in the conference itself. Our Chairman was a delightful Professor from Australia who loved a good story to start a tough presentation. It so happened that for the first time we had a delegate from China who brought with him an interpreter. A joke is a great way to start a tough programme so Barry told us of an Australian who, on a hot day, was sitting on the porch, or veranda, of his house, when a casual labourer asked if he had any odd jobs which needed doing and he said, "Yes, go round the back of the house and paint the porch with the tin of red paint there." The odd job man returned a couple of hours later to be paid, and as he left said, "Oh, by the way, it isn't a Porsche, it is a Ferrari."

The best laugh, perhaps unkindly, was watching the interpreter explain the joke in Chinese. Later Barry recognised the badge I had in my lapel, and I noticed he had the same one: Scripture Union. We shared the aim of spending time daily with a brief Bible reading.

My own interest was directed to the way Americans used objective, or multiple-choice, questions. In Britain we traditionally scorned this mechanistic approach, but since we in Scotland were embarking on raising the school-leaving age for all pupils at sixteen, it meant we needed to include a wider range of ability and assessments in the terminal exams for them. The Americans had approached a similar problem by using a lot of machine-marked, multiple-choice questions and "turning statistics into information" as the catch phrase put it. I went home with a figure of 30% in my mind as a maximum proportion of multiple-choice questions in our exams for sixteen year olds.

These yearly overseas trips always had unique elements to them. We met in Dublin not long after Eire joined, what was then called, the Common Market and I asked our host what particularly attracted his countrymen and his answer was simple: "If you found a fella who promised that for every pound you gave him, he would give you two back, what would you say?" Simple! If only all political issues had such an easy solution.

## Other IAEA Meetings: Montreal

Montreal was memorable in another way. I had Canadian siblings who had lived there but were no longer with us and indeed I had briefly worked in a tea company prior to going to university, but this time I had a wife and Hilda was able to do interesting things while we at the conference were occupied. We had flown into Montreal via Boston and planned to do a little travelling on our way home. We rented a car and took a leisurely trip to Boston via Harvard University and Martha's Vineyard. One of the delegates was the son of a previous Master (Warden ?) of Harvard and he insisted on giving us a conducted tour of the University and also directing us to points of interest en route which we would never have known. He also had a taste in wine which made for a memorable lunch.

We finished the trip by going to Martha's Vineyard which was interesting for two contrasting things: it was the playground of the Kennedy family on Chappaquiddick Island and notorious for the death of Mary-Jo Kopechne when in a car driven by Teddy Kennedy (brother of John Kennedy) which drove off a bridge into the sea. The exact details of the accident were a matter of endless press curiosity.

Elsewhere there was something very different: a quaint open-air meeting place with a central wrought iron structure like a Victorian band stand and a circle of small cottages built in the quaint 'gingerbread' style where the basic structure is decorated with additional panels carved in shapes and colours of the builder's choice. Christian families would gather for a week of hymn-singing, match-making and holiday combined with some rousing rustic preaching.

## Beijing, Hong Kong, Australia and Fji

My IAEA meetings took a more formal shape in1989 when we were due to meet in China and, of course, in Beijing (I wondered if the Chinese delegate and his interpreter had managed to work out the Iowa joke about the porch.) Plans were fairly well forward when there were the unfortunate events in Tiananmen Square, so the conference was postponed and the Australians kindly agreed to host the meeting at Bondi beach near Sydney. The new date neatly coincided with the retirement of Dr Farquhar Macintosh, who for many years had been Chairman of the Exam Board. It was agreed that as an appreciation of his commitment to the Board and its work, he would attend the Sydney meeting. As the plans were made, so also they developed. Mrs Macintosh was also retiring after years as the Head Teacher of a big Edinburgh comprehensive school, so it was arranged that we would be a party of three, with me in my usual role at the IAEA and general factotum to see that all went well – as it did.

We paid a fraternal visit to the authorities in Kuala Lumpur in Malaysia and then went on to Hong Kong. As it happened, the Macintoshes knew the last British Governor of Hong Kong and by a strange coincidence he was the brother-in-law of the minister of the church I attended in Scotland. In fact, our hostess was the Governor's wife, whom we met for morning coffee in the Governor's residence just a short time before the Governor brought to an end Britain's long association with the island.

From there we went on to Sydney for the IAEA part of the tour and stayed in a hotel just above Bondi beach. Hard by the hotel was a very large graveyard and as I strolled round looking at headstones and names, I gradually realised that large parts of the space were taken up by defunct Irish immigrants, yet there was a fascinating feature of the place. A wide space went between the burials and soon it was clear that the O'Hallorans, Kellys and O'Shaughnessies were on one side and the MacGregors, Rosses and Smiths were on the other. As in life, so in death: "No Surrender". The Protestants and Catholics died as they lived, yielding "no surrender" to the other party – even on the other side of the world.

The initial planning of the trip scheduled a direct flight from Sydney to Los Angeles where there would be a parting of the ways, but at short notice the Mackintoshes felt it would be a shame not to see at least one Pacific Island, so I negotiated a change of tickets so that we could spend a few days in Fiji. The trouble was that when we arrived, not a single hotel had any spare accommodation, such was the demand of the holiday season. It so happened that a dear friend of mine was the Director of Scripture Union in Fiji and they just happened to have a guest house that was un-occupied: problem solved. I eventually left my charges in Los Angeles as they flew on to their appointments, and I to see my Canadian/American relatives.

## IAEA – New Zealand

It had to come eventually: IAEA was hosted by the New Zealanders who (probably because of their largely Scottish ancestors), were innovators in educational matters. There has always been a gulf in education between those young people who are, for lack of a better word, 'academic' as opposed to those whose abilities are in more practical skills, to the detriment of the latter. A common certification for both groups, academic and practical, would also be part of the New Zealand scheme. Scottish Standard grade exams did a lot to correct that, since all candidates did the same exam, albeit at different levels.

At the other end of the world the Kiwis were looking at the similar division in the post-school gap between university and vocational qualifications and it was that event which took us to New Zealand. Technical

Colleges were upgrading to be universities and many academic universities were developing in technical areas. It was a recognition of a changing world, and soon the same problems were finding matching solutions in Britain.

On the professional side of things, the conference was a stimulus for all participants about a changing world and I went home to discuss what lay ahead at the Exam Board.

On a personal level. everyone in Scotland has antipodean relatives and we were no exception. Hilda's father, John, had a younger brother, Jim, and they had interesting similarities and very marked differences. Both had excellent bass voices and performed duets on social and spiritual occasions. John, Hilda's Dad, was industrious, cautious, conventional and went into insurance, with considerable success in persuading farmers in the north of Scotland to exercise their traditional prudence by taking out life policies.

Uncle Jim was totally different. He was a second-generation missionary to what is now Zambia and was then Northern Rhodesia. He got there by canoe up the Zambezi River and built his own home. For many years he did a regular broadcast on the national radio singing a daily hymn. I think he it was who spotted the hymn, *O Lord my God, when I in awesome wonder*, and popularised it in his daily broadcast. Jim was a pioneer. His daughter Jean, trained as a nurse in Britain and there got to know the Scottish side of the family, but she eventually retired to New Zealand to be near her married children. We made contact on arrival in Wellington and Hilda and she talked non-stop for most of two days, aware of the uniqueness of the occasion.

While Hilda was remembering her links with her cousin Jean, I was deep in recollection with Ronald Fountain, a classmate from school days in Ooty. En route to New Zealand we stopped off in India.

## India

We checked into a city-centre hotel in Delhi where a magnificent Sikh Sergeant Major, bedecked with sash and medals, came smartly attention with a stamp of his feet, saluted and said, "Welcome to Delhi." After dinner we took a stroll round the block before bed-time and something nudged Hilda in the back. To her surprise it was a lonely cow browsing on whatever patches of grass there might be found at ten o'clock in the middle of a capital city. En route to Agra and the Taj Mahal the next morning she was shocked to see shrouded dead bodies lined up on the pavement, presumably for burial that day, until the 'corpses' got up, ready for a day's work. Welcome to India.

What is there to say about the Taj Mahal that has not been said? In a way, the events of the day and the one following summed up something of India's essence. Side by side with fabulous wealth, artistic perfection, technical skill of the highest order went abject poverty, with a whole caste system that effectively traps individuals with little chance to move out of it. But the other side of that caste system was evident in the numerous salesmen who urged us to buy a picnic table which was made with the same materials and inlaid with the semi-precious stones that decorated the Taj Mahal, and they were made by the descendants of the technicians who originally decorated the tomb. It perfectly illustrated the continuance of the caste system across the centuries. The only downside was an attack of 'Delhi-belly' for Hilda, but there is always a statistical likelihood of that happening, even in the best hotels. We put it down to traveller's experience.

## Omsk, Siberia – British Council

Dostoevsky was exiled to Omsk and so were a great many other people from time to time. I had a number of reasons to go to Russia around that time, but they took me to Moscow: Siberia had very different associations. mostly unpleasant ones. Siberia itself suggested endless forest and tundra, a place of exile and punishment, so why go there? The answer was the British Council, which is an admirable branch of the Foreign Office and exists to spread quiet influence and awareness of how British institutions can help other countries, and indeed most western countries have similar organisations.

From a personal point of view it seems that when you have done one job for the Council, there may be others if you have not made a complete mess of the first. My work with the Egyptians obviously played a part, so here I was travelling to Moscow by British Airways and then to a Russian plane for the next long leg. The contrast could not have been more startling. Yes, it was a plane; yes, it was a jet plane, but the take off was startling. I was familiar, from RAF days, with the rate of climb in an elderly piston-engined Dakota, such as I flew in for National service, but that was double the rate of this elderly cargo plane with minimal refinements. It lumbered off the runway – just, by skimming the boundary fence and then staggered to flying height.

A stewardess came round with a trolley, but imagine a very wobbly version of something your grandmother might have used. There was vodka – or vodka – and my suggestion of a soft drink just didn't register. We parted in mutual bafflement.

I noticed that the doors of some overhead lockers were closed – but not all, and no one bothered to close them.

There were some safety belts, but not on mine; my seat had a base and a back, but each moved independently of the other. You could have both down or both up or one in each direction. I found that both wooden parts of the seat rotated on a sturdy steel bar bolted to the floor. Development and expense of passenger flying were low on the list for government spending and needless to say there was no private investment in internal flying.

I was met at the airport and taken to my accommodation, which turned out to be a 'prophilactorium', which probably needs some explanation. If a 'sanitorium' is a place which make you sane, or healthy, a prophilactorium stops you from getting ill: simple. I gathered that workers, under the old communist system, who deserved a reward for their conscientious labour, could be given the privilege of a week or more in pleasant surroundings. I actually never saw these rewards but I guessed they took a healthy, hearty kind of exercise and relaxation. My colleague Lucy and I found the breakfast to be healthy but unappealing. It was March when we were there and obviously fruit and vegetables were in short supply, and most food seemed to start as milk and then go sour. The staff were astonished – and said so – when any food was returned un-eaten. That really let the side down.

Our appointment was with the Professor and staff of the University of Omsk and the early comment of the Professor of English will always remain in my mind. She said in flawless English, "I know that in your culture it 'isn't done' to talk about money: we talk about nothing else." To explain, this was the point in Russian history when Gorbachev's attempt to reform and reorganise the Soviet economy was about to fail. Thereafter there was an attempt by Yeltsin to lead the country out of collapse. The staff each said that they had three or four jobs of some kind in an attempt to survive. The Professor and her son shared her mother's house.

The next surprise came out of a clear blue sky. The British Council, in their wisdom, had given us two new computers for the Department which I set up and one of the staff brought a disk and asked me how to up-load it. The first words that appeared were, "Dear Sister in Christ!"

"Are you a Christian", I asked.

"Yes, are you?"

Her story was that as a student there had been a visit to the city by a group of young British evangelists, and she had come to faith through them. I asked if she attended the Orthodox Church, but that got a brisk denial. No, there was a lively Evangelical Church which met every Sunday in a local Technical College for a lot of lively singing and preaching and much more to the taste of local young people. It had never occurred to me that such things were tolerated under the Communist system. It was more likely that in the political turmoil at the time that no-one neither knew nor cared.

We came back for a second visit and this time the weather had changed and the first signs of spring were appearing. A hotel existed which had previously been for the exclusive use of Party Officials on big business, and in my innocence of such places I couldn't understand what was said by women who phoned and said something un-intelligible. On the fourth or fifth call I said something irritable and explained that I didn't speak Russian.

"Sex, Sex" was the reply. Some words cross all linguistic barriers.

On this trip we were entertained to a small, formal dinner by the senior leaders in the Ministry of Education. The food was much better. The milk derivatives had gone and there was some very fine steak. Sadly, we had no Russian and they had no English, but we beamed at each other in a fraternal way.

Russians describe their country as "Moscow – and everything else". There are two tall, skyscrapers built in red sandstone in the middle of Moscow and on our second trip we stayed about halfway up one of these as we waited for a return flight. Between our initial flight at the end of winter and this trip in early May, first of all the plane had changed. Gone was the decrepit cold-war relic that got us to Omsk – just. Instead, we flew in and out on a modern European plane, which was at the same time a huge relief, but there was just the memory of something honest about Russia and the economy at that time. Moscow was becoming something like a western city with a tourist centre that might have been – anywhere – but we were assured that the rest of Russia, the real Russia was much as it had always been. Yet inside that economic collapse people were still driving the Trabants and Ladas that poured off the production lines, in contrast to the stolen Mercedes and Jaguars that crawled the Moscow streets.

There was a sequel to the Russian trip when the British Council in their generosity invited the Professor to come to Scotland to establish our contacts with the excellent people in the Omsk English Department. I particularly remember that she stayed in a hotel in the centre of Edinburgh just opposite the Usher Hall where concerts were held. There was a general air of prosperity and cultural life. Her face was a study as various emotions crossed her face and as she expressed what the visit meant to her. I thought of the 'prophilactorium' and the milk diet in my first visit, and the collapsed economy of the post-Gorbachev times. She loved Britain and the English language, but she also profoundly loved her own country, despite the upheavals of a collapsing economy.

**Eritrea**

I got a request from the British Council to go to Eritrea.

I knew very little about Eritrea when I got the invitation or about the current situation. In the previous eleven years the country had fought a bitter and, eventually, successful war against Ethiopia and their educational system was looking to develop as far as their situation allowed.

In our new exams, we had tried to develop problem-solving skills, based on life experiences, like calculating the number of bricks in the gable end of a building, or the length of the groove on a long-playing record. (I am not sure how many people might actually care about the results, but you get the principle behind it.)

I quickly got the highest opinion of my hosts. The leadership of the country during the war lived almost permanently underground, for fear of Ethiopian bombing. In a huge network of caves, they developed their schools, their justice system, their medical practice almost from scratch. But I had the highest admiration for what they did with the railway system. To understand, a look at a map would help, but essentially, the country is on a plateau some 5,000 feet above sea level, where the capital, Asmara, is situated. The main port on the Red Sea is reached by a steep road and also a railway built after the second world war. In the war against Ethiopia the railway was dug up and the sleepers used for gun emplacements and obstacles against attack from the sea. After the war various European countries offered to replace it – at a price. Instead, they rebuilt the railway line themselves and restored two diesel engines – with minimal hard currency.

This spirit of can-do independence impressed me greatly at the time.

The group of teachers and administrators I spoke to were eager to accept and try for themselves anything that might be applicable to their schools, and indeed there could not have been more fertile soil to speak about solving real life problems.

But there was a lingering sadness running through my time there and that was the permanent state of tension between themselves and the rest of Ethiopia and the likelihood it could flare up again. The tendency towards authoritarian presidents seems to be a recurring weakness.

One personal story sticks in my mind. He was called Peter and after ten years of war he got a scholarship to do a year's study in Britain. Before the war he had become separated from his son, who also got funding to study in Europe. With great difficulty they arranged to meet – specifically in King's Cross Station at a particular time. Peter was in position and watched as the passengers came through the ticket gate but saw no sign of his son. As he explained it to me, he turned away sadly and as he walked toward the exit a black man came up and said, "Are you my father?" Neither had recognised the other. That is what war does.

## Zimbabwe

My first visit to Zimbabwe was in 1984, to a conference of Scripture Union leaders from several countries, called by the International Secretary, Nigel Sylvester. I checked to see if he merited a mention in Google, but the name brought up a champion BMX cyclist rather than my old friend. Nigel got a first in Maths at Cambridge, but rather than pursue an academic career he devoted his life to the young people of Ghana through the work of Scripture Union. His colleague, John Dean, did similar work in Nigeria. Large numbers of young people came to faith through their work. The situation in South Africa was quite different. Churches were still in the grip of apartheid, and to some degree that applied in SU's youth work. Black young people were not thought to have the leadership potential necessary to lead a national movement. The quality of leaders from Nigeria and Ghana were a revelation to the South Africans. One white leader said to me, "None of our 'boys' could be like that," to which the obvious question was, "Why not?"

One purpose of the conference was to persuade all the African movements to expand their activities. At the end of the conference there was a great hope that expansion into the communist countries might take place before the next conference seven years later.

1987 was an interesting year for those with an interest in Russia. The Orthodox Church celebrated its millennium, looking back to a group of

Byzantine monks who came up the Dnieper river to establish the Orthodox faith .

In 1987 the Communist Party in Russia celebrated seventy years since the October revolution. And then the following year the Berlin Wall came down. Well, Communism lasted longer than Hitler's 'Thousand year Reich'.

## Zimbabwe Again

The second time I went to Zimbabwe, it was at the request of the Ministry of Education in Britain who wanted a review of the use of examinations prepared and marked by the Cambridge Schools Examination Board. For many years, going back to the Empire days, Cambridge had prepared and administered school-leaving exams for children throughout the English-speaking world and thereby established standards equivalent to what was happening in Britain.

This was 1993 in the days of Robert Mugabe when the outside world had applied sanctions to his regime and essentially left the country to its own devices. However, Cambridge exams were still used by schools who hoped that some of their pupils could use the results to move on to higher education abroad. The question was, why should the British tax-payer subsidise a regime which resisted all attempts to abide by the norms of the wider world? Perhaps they should produce their own exams and offer them for evaluation. I also suspected, with good reason, that Zimbabwe were letting children take Cambridge exams, but didn't pay the fees for lack of foreign currency.

On a personal level it was a joy to visit and stay with old friends in Harare, some of them black and a few white who in, a very committed way respected and lived within the conditions of Zimbabwean citizenship.

My reception at the exam authority was not joyfully enthusiastic. The Minister was out of town; the Director of the Education authority was not available and what was the purpose of my visit? I had written in advance and so had Cambridge. I spoke to individual members of the Ministry who showed less than no enthusiasm for independence from Cambridge.

I wrote a report of my conclusions, outlining the essentials of setting up an examination process and really saying that there was neither the desire nor the expertise required.

A second meeting put another angle on the same problem. I had a meal with good friends in Harare and after the meal another friend came in. He was the manager for an international electronics company and he needed some ten thousand US dollars to cover his bills. He went to the Zimbabwe exchequer to get the money. He was told, "There is no money: no money in the exchequer", and equally no appetite for an independent examination system.

It was tragic to see the decline of a wealthy country, the 'bread basket of Africa', slump into apathy. Inter-national sanctions, as always, seemed to hit the weakest and the poorest in the country.

## Primary School Testing in Scotland

My last job at the Exam Board was to introduce Primary School testing throughout Scotland in English and Mathematics. The idea came from Mrs Thatcher, the Prime Minister at the time, who had been convinced that the Nation needed a firm grasp of the basics: but which Nation? That was the rub. Quite soon after the political announcement I was a lamb to the slaughter of a televised discussion about the wisdom and the desirability of the policy. There were impassioned speeches from representatives of the Teachers' Unions all denouncing this retreat into mindless rote learning, and anyway who was Maggie Thatcher to tell the Educational Institute of Scotland's representatives what was good for the weans. And then some impassioned mothers leapt to the defence of the same weans and insisted that they "only wanted the weans to be happy in school".

My defence was that I was just a simple functionary whose role was to implement government policy and not necessarily to defend it. However, I did my bit to explain that the tests would not be like tests as parents might remember them. There was not a whiff of the infamous eleven plus tests which divided children into two groups that would never meet again. Instead, these tests would be humane and indeed administered in such a way that the children would not know they were being tested at all. How was this slight of hand to be arranged?

Very simply, we would develop and produce these tests at five levels labelled from A to E where A was for beginners and E for the oldest. They would be administered whenever the teacher thought it appropriate. I remember doing battle with fiery teachers from the Black Isle to Galloway and gradually the row subsided and there were favourable comments in many quarters.

The next stage was to produce these tests in vast quantities for distribution as required, and I made friends with printers across the country, inevitably ending up with tried and tested firms who knew the business well. And there was a happy accident of timing for the digital revolution was just about to break out. Eventually we simply gave teachers master copies of tests and left them to print and administer the tests as and when they thought pupils were ready.

There was a sequel to all this. In England, after a great deal of political uproar much as in Scotland, it was agreed that there would be primary testing, but in a way suitable to the politics. Just for fun I applied and went with a colleague to an interview. Our argument was strong and indeed we had done it. The evidence was laid in front of the interviewing members of the Department of Education. At the end of my presentation, the Chairman said, "I cannot argue with you: you could do it perfectly well – but it is, as you know, quite impossible for Scotland to teach us in England how to conduct a national test. Thank you and good bye!"

It was good fun.

## Other travel – Kalimpong

The 'Hill Stations' of North India have developed an extensive literature through writers like Rudyard Kipling, Jim Corbett and other writers on British rule in India, with Darjeeling and Simla the best known. Kalimpong was less well known but it was a centre for Christian missionaries and tea planters in the second half of the nineteenth century. Well known in India is the school started by a Dr Graham who established a school for Anglo-Indian children. They were often neglected by both their parents' communities. Many of them were the children of railway engineers and drivers, since jobs on the railways were often reserved for the Anglo-Indian community. Initially the school provided an excellent education for orphans and the graduates travelled all over the world. A former pupils' association supports the school in many ways so that others can have the benefits they had.

Alongside the school there is a thriving church, now part of the Church of North India. There are continual fraternal links with the Church of Scotland, since it was Scottish missionaries who first established a church at the end of the nineteenth century. Along with friends from our home church I visited Kalimpong and was enormously impressed with the thriving congregation and the schools which developed from earlier missionaries. Similarly, the hospital has served the wider community very well with dedicated staff. Originally there was a hospital for lepers but thankfully that has not been needed for many years, such is the progress treatment for the disease. There are sublime views across to Bhutan.

The tea plantations immediately took me back to the Nilgiri Hills of my birth, but the thing that struck me most was the results of Kalimpong's unique climate. I have a collection of pictures of the largest collection of varied fungi I have ever seen.

## Moving On

Shortly after this, I handed in my resignation at the Exam Board. We had been through ten years of national change; there was every prospect that the new system was bedding in and was producing good teaching and learning, but my personal question was, what next? Our boys, Ashley and Barry, had moved through Balerno High School to University, Ashley to do Engineering and teaching and Barry to Media Studies and then a job in Glasgow and later the BBC in London.

As parents we were increasingly redundant. By the mid-nineties we felt my time at the Exam Board was coming to an end. Our boys were increasingly independent, and weddings were under discussion so the question was, what next?

# 7 Scripture Union

Scripture Union runs like a thread through my life. Earlier I mentioned my early days at school in the Nilgiri Hills when we had a regular visit from Cecil Johnston, a travelling Secretary, who worked his way around India doing missions in boarding schools, including Breeks, where I was a pupil. John Jacob, my housemaster, later worked for SU in Scotland and India and our paths crossed many times since my primary school days.

Scripture Union began by accident on a beach at Llandudno, in North Wales when a man called Josiah Spiers saw some bored children and stopped to write words in the sand. When curious ones gathered round, he invited them to decorate the words with seaweed and stones. When complete the drawing spelt out the words, "God is love". As he said goodbye to the children one asked, "What time will you be here tomorrow?" and that started the first beach mission. That is the 'creation myth' of SU.

In 1879, the Children's Scripture Union, a system of daily Bible reading was started. A membership card had a list of daily readings, and this was soon complemented by explanatory notes in children's magazines. These two strands of Bible reading and services that children might actually enjoy, found expression in increasing numbers of countries leading to the modern movement which embraces work in more than 120 different countries.

### Statement of Faith

*Working with the churches, Scripture Union aims to:*

- *make God's Good News known to children, young people and families, and*
- *encourage people of all ages to meet God daily through the Bible and prayer,*
- *so that they may come to personal faith in our Lord Jesus Christ, grow in Christian maturity and become both committed church members and servants of a world in need.*

*Scripture Union pursues these aims through a variety of ministries around the world in obedience to our Lord Jesus Christ in reliance on the Holy Spirit.*

For many years Hilda and I had had different kinds of involvement with SU. As a teenager she had been to SU holidays and had worked as a cook at various events. Before we had children, we led an SU skiing holiday at an outdoor centre in the Cairngorms, with a fairly dramatic outcome. We had a group of about a dozen teenage boys. On the second day we were on the slopes at Glenshee in early afternoon when there was a warning to get off the slopes as soon as possible, so we did, just as a blizzard came down, making it difficult to make it back to where we were staying.

As we arrived, the Warden said, "We have just had a phone call from the ski centre that one of your group is lying on the hill with a broken leg." A headcount showed that all our boys were present and correct – except my co-leader who had remained on the slopes for a last run with some friends and had broken his leg. Quite apart from the problems of getting him down to safety and treatment, he was meant to do much of the instruction.

We also got involved in sailing holidays for teenagers, in cooperation with our in-laws, Bob and Marion Craig, who lived in Campbeltown almost at the end of the Kintyre peninsula, looking across to Ireland. Bob was a passionate sailor and with his boat and a couple of others, we arranged to fill two or three boats with young people for sailing holidays up the west coast of Scotland to the inner Hebrides and, weather permitting, as far as Skye. Hilda and her sister Marion provisioned the boats.

These were formative years for many youngsters – and ourselves. The format was simple: a short thought for the day from the Bible after breakfast; a day's sailing in marvellous scenery and sometimes weather to match, and in the evening a brief talk and open discussion on basic aspects of the gospel – and life. Usually, we would have three boats, which would give a maximum number of twelve or thirteen youngsters.

I treasure many memories of these holidays, one of which was unique. Each day the boats would anchor at one of the inner Hebrides and on this occasion it was Eigg, which has a very distinctive profile, like a great wedge of cheese, which ends in a cliff called An Sgurr, a dramatic pitchstone ridge, the largest of its kind in Europe.

I was standing right on the Sgurr when I looked up and saw an aerial battle between two birds – a sea eagle and a peregrine falcon. The sea eagles had been introduced to Eigg some years before and were still an uncommon sight, but so too were the peregrines and to see both in serious action was a privilege for a non-ornithologist. I have seen spitfire dog fights on war films but that was small beer by comparison with those two birds. The sea eagles were a recent addition to Scottish Islands and the peregrine's ancestors had arrived a long time before, so any intruder was in for a fight. They were still fighting as they moved out of sight.

It was an enormous privilege to take young people on these cruises and it was a first experience for many. The west coast of Scotland has innumerable anchorages in majestic scenery – and also unpredictable weather. A week's cruise could expect a variety of weathers and possibly a night in an anchorage with a gale blowing out at sea.

But the west coast is also full of dramatic stories based on real events and people. There is a famous poem by Thomas Campbell that goes like this:

A Chieftain to the Highlands bound cries, "Boatman, do not tarry!
And I'll give thee a silver pound, to row us o'er the ferry."

"Now who be ye, would cross Lochgyle, this dark and stormy water?"
"O, I'm the chief of Ulva's isle, and this Lord Ullin's daughter.

"And fast before her father's men three days we've fled together,
And should they find us in this glen, my blood would stain the heather."

Naturally, young love meets a tragic end and father bewails his stubborn pride – but too late.

I learnt this poem at school and it stuck in my mind until one day on one of the sailing cruises we arrived at the Island – of Ulva – and the poem came back to me. I imagined these star-crossed lovers eloping from an angry father and perishing in the stormy waters.

Later I learnt that the ancestors of a good friend *had* lived and farmed on Ulva. Their story also was unhappy, but in a different way. In the nineteenth century the old clan system of land ownership and tenant farming, became uneconomic and landlords evicted their tenants in what was called the Highland Clearances. Thousands of landless people emigrated to various parts of the British Empire and eventually, after great hardships, these emigrants took their energy, their thrift and their skills to Canada, Australia, New Zealand. My friend's ancestor was driven off his land but fortunately found a more gracious and generous landlord elsewhere in Scotland.

These sailing holidays introduced to young people the history and geography of their native land and put the Gospel of Jesus in a wider context as well as being a lot of fun. Holidays are a great big learning experience.

## International Scripture Union

As a result of my links with SU, starting in childhood in India, I was asked to be Chairman of SU Scotland which I did for a number of years. This involved meetings with the leaders of England and Ireland and also the worldwide movement. SU had grown greatly in Africa, mainly through the work of a couple of outstanding men. Nigel Sylvester and John Dean, both Cambridge graduates, who had worked for many years in Ghana and Nigeria respectively. When Nigel was International Director, he convened an International Conference in Harare, Zimbabwe in 1984; the second of its kind. He wanted the international movement to catch a vision for growth of the kind that he had seen in Africa. It was a life-changing event for many people. On the last afternoon, there were the beginnings of a plan to develop SU behind the 'Iron Curtain'.

I have expressed it in these terms because that reflected the feeling about Russia and the Communist countries at that time. The phrase was Churchill's when he said that after World War Two it was as though a great barrier, an iron curtain, had developed between the Western democracies and the Communist countries of Eastern Europe. The thought of tiny SU planting in the forbidding territories of communism seemed unlikely.

In 1988 communism collapsed, and in 1989 the Berlin wall, which divided Europe between communist and other western countries, was demolished.

Shortly after, SU began work in Ukraine in cooperation with an energetic Baptist called Grigori Stupak. His story was interesting. His father, a Baptist Minister, had been given ten years in one of Stalin's labour camps which were so powerfully described in Alexander Solzhenitsyn's books. Towards the end of his ten years, Stalin died in 1953; there was a more relaxed attitude in the camp and a few trusted prisoners were allowed to bring in their wives, including Grigori's parents. And that was how Grigori was born in a labour camp. Grigori was central to the development of SU in Ukraine and other parts of Russia.

Our main contact in setting up SU in Russia was a man who had made an academic study of Evangelical churches in Russia which was published under the title *Russian Resurrection – A history of Russia's Evangelical Church* by Michael Rowe. Michael's knowledge of Communist Russia and the wider Communist countries was second to none. As absolute beginners, the little group who were trying to find our way into the Communist world, we needed someone with pioneering gifts and that eventually was Danilo Gay. At the time, Danilo was leading SU in Quebec province of Canada. He was admirably gifted for the job, since he was from French-speaking Switzerland but also spoke flawless English. These were not necessarily ideal for pioneering in Russia, but he was a pioneer. Gradually, the possibilities for starting SU were emerging and the way forward was to offer to churches the expertise SU had developed in children's work where the need was unlimited, since children do not normally play much part in church services.

In due course, I found myself with four other SU friends arriving at Kyiv airport with $10,000 tucked into my socks and each of my friends had the same. This was not in any sense illegal: it was to avoid the attentions of the mafia who would otherwise have been looking for a share.

On our first Sunday we went to a Baptist church in Kyiv and it was a shock.. I had a mental image of persecuted people meeting in fear of police intervention. What I saw was a church packed to the last seat. Indeed, people got up to offer their seats to the visitors. The singing was extraordinary, particularly from two contralto women soloists whose voices had a power and a unique quality that was thrilling to hear.

The Baptist Churches in Ukraine and Russia were started by a combination of disillusionment with the Orthodox Church and German exiles who refused to conform to the national church in Germany in the 19th century. They did not escape persecution in Russia either, particularly from the Cossacks, but they had grown over the years into a substantial numbers of churches.

Grigori was our man in Ukraine: our man in Russia was a very different character. Andrei was an engineer on the Russian space programme. As a student he had met and married a fellow student but after a time they divorced and went their separate ways. Karena had a very similar early marriage which had ended in divorce. They met some years later and knew they wished to be together, but Karina was clear that, as she put it, she wanted God in their marriage. As good Communists this was a novelty and it was with great reluctance that Andrei agreed to be baptised as the pre-requisite for marriage in the Orthodox Church, but he had one condition: it had to be done by Father Alexander Men.

This priest was well known in Moscow as a vigorous critic, equally of the Orthodox Church and the Communist government, but he would not marry anyone who had not been baptised into the Church. Other priests might be persuaded to ignore this condition or would perform a perfunctory ceremony just before the wedding. It got worse. Father Alexander would only baptise Andrei if he first attended six weekly baptismal classes. Love prevailed and a very dejected Andrei turned up to the first class with a good many other candidates.

The shock came at the end of the sixth talk when Father Alexander said, "Now Andrei is going to tell you how all this theological knowledge is transformed into a living faith: when the head activates the heart." Panic! How could he speak of something which had not happened? He started talking but could never remember what he said. He only knew that when he sat down something life-changing had happened.

When he mentioned his faith at work, he lost his job with the Russian space project.

Father Alexander's story was rather more dramatic. One day as he walked from his church to his home a man stepped out from behind a fence and split his head open with an axe. The assassin was never found, but there was one strange feature of the crime, which may have been a coincidence. The day of the murder was the day when the Orthodox Church celebrated the feast of John the Baptist, who, as you will recall, had his head chopped off.

Andrei was a man who simply loved the Bible – and was prepared to lose his job in the process. Karina, his wife, was his partner in every sense. He was a great help in enabling SU to understand Russian culture and society.

With these early contacts a way forward was beginning to emerge, and we saw that SU could contribute to Russian churches with its experience in children's ministry. Gradually publicity about conferences spread and one of the early enthusiasts was from Armenia. Vardan was a member of an evangelical wing of the Arminian Orthodox church who had a passion for reaching young people. His first effort was to run a two-week holiday club for children and it was such a success that the mayor of the town gave his full support and made a piece of land available for their activities. Later they were able to put a building on the site for use for meetings and related activities. Elsewhere seminars on children's work encouraged and inspired churches to develop their own congregations.

Let me go back to my first visit to Ukraine, with the $10,000 in my socks and the four other colleagues with the same amount in theirs. Our contacts in Ukraine through Michael Rowe had a big vision. Their work with teenagers and others had developed to the point where they wished to start something like the outdoor holiday events which are such a feature of SU in Britain and elsewhere. To cut a very long story to manageable proportions, Grigori had identified a piece of land with an existing building on it which could provide indoor and outdoor activities not just for young people but also for adult conferences. Nearby there was a lake where water sports were possible and in due course the property was bought and has been in excellent use ever since.

For most of this time I was still working for the Scottish Examination Board, but also encouraging friends and congregations to support developments in Ukraine and Russia as best I could and I have one particular event which continues to keep me humble.

Danilo Gay, our Swiss man in Russia, was on a visit to Scotland and with him we went to a number of places where churches and individuals might undertake to pray and support work in Ukraine. On one occasion we visited a town which I will not mention, to spare my blushes rather than theirs. Before we spoke, another potential fund-raiser had spoken enthusiastically about his work and when he had finished I introduced Danilo who presented the work in Ukraine. Watching the faces of the audience I did not feel encouraged as we drove away and I said so to Danilo.

I could not have been more wrong. There was a young man who ran a pancake restaurant in the town and also had an SU group in his church. Every year since then he has taken a group of young people to Ukraine and that was well over twenty years ago. This contact has been a huge benefit to both ends of the relationship. The Scottish young people have a rare opportunity to meet their Ukrainian contemporaries and there have been return visits to Scotland by the Ukrainians.

The land purchased at Vorzel is close to a site that is internationally notorious: Chernobyl. The atomic power station that spread radio-active particles across vast areas of the earth is now encased in a concrete shell. It is nice to think that power of another kind is spread generously in the lives of young people.

Before the recent war in Ukraine, I had an email from Grigori saying that they had their 2,000[th] young person at their summer events there with the usual SU combination of outdoor activities and sharing the Good News.

Meanwhile in St Petersburg, Danilo had found another enthusiast for Christian work among young people. Her name was Vera Zhuravleva. After the collapse of Communism in 1988, St Petersburg was two very different places. There was the waterfront area where the cruise ships arrived to bring wealthy Europeans to the city built by the Czars, with the Hermitage Museum, and the Winter Palace, but the city behind the waterfront was very different, with the standard, cheap, basic apartments for the labouring poor. After 1988 there was widespread poverty and that was the area where Vera worked. For Vera, the Gospel is both spiritual and material and helping the poorest to survive in winter was a priority. She opened the office or Bible room in St Petersburg's and that became a centre for Bible studies and a base for reaching young people on the streets, many with addictions.

The house she got in a rural area was used initially for summer camps but became much more of a local centre for families with children who had additional needs. She had the support of a very sympathetic local Orthodox priest. The other side of her work was a cottage she had been given in the north of Russia, near the city of Murmansk where she combined a holiday for poor families with the Good News. When Communism collapsed many Christians emigrated from Russia to more tolerant countries like the USA and Canada, including her family. Vera decided to stay and remains, committed to the care of the many small people who need her.

## SU England and Wales (1996 –20021)

In 1996 I decided that it was time to leave the Exam Board. I felt that Standard Grade and Primary Assessment were up and running, so when there was a vacancy for a CEO at Scripture Union in England and Wales, I applied. SUEW had been going for 150 years with a publishing arm and a team of people who supported SU's work in schools and ran an extensive programme of holiday missions and camps for young people of various ages.

On the International side of SU I had seen a good many national movements across the world, but would long-established SU England take kindly to a foreigner and especially one from Scotland.? I have always argued that I am one of the few genuinely British people I know, since I have an English father, an Irish mother, a Scottish wife and was born in a large part of the British Empire. I couldn't claim any Welsh blood, but no one is perfect. Consequently, I felt free from any particular national bias. In brief, I was appointed.

We moved to the lovely Milton Keynes while there were still jokes about the concrete cows. If this means nothing to you, pass on. Yes, MK was a new town and the object of a certain kind of sneering, which quickly disappeared if you actually lived there. I guess it was the only place in England where you never got caught in a traffic jam; where you could always park at a supermarket; and it had its own indoor ski slope.

I had a great management team with two old SU hands in John Grayston and Leslie Blight and another new boy, in Andrew Stockbridge. John had been in SU forever in a variety of roles and managed our publishing, and Leslie managed all our field staff who were out working with schools or holidays. Andrew covered administration and finance, and came with high and justified commendation.

The Chairman of SU, John Simmonds, was very excited about the international side of SU, since attending the second conference held in Maastricht, Holland in 1994 and was keen to encourage and support the worldwide movement. This fitted very well with my own interests and together we considered how that could be done, but there was also an issue nearer home.

At one time there was just Scripture Union, as it was called, a single entity that was a Bible reading organisation. As it developed in different parts of the world and in different languages, it also increased the range of activities beyond Bible reading and beach missions into camping and activity holidays. Initially in Britain there was just – SU, but when Scotland felt well enough established to run their own show, SU Scotland was born and it seemed that movements thrived when they had a national identity, so how about SU Wales, rather than SUEW? Were there people who might see that as a personal challenge?

I can't remember just how it came about but I contacted a number of Christian groups who were concerned about teenagers and I spoke to one person who visibly bristled when I raised the idea of a separate SU movement for Wales. In brief he challenged me to come and listen to his view as a Welshman, rather than tell him what my vision might be. I spent twenty-four hours listening to what he said, and it began with the following statement: "You will never understand the Welsh until you realise that we are a defeated nation imprisoned in our own land."

At the end of twenty-four hours I think I understood very well what he wanted and to some degree we could cooperate. I invited him to join a committee and when I got his application form it included the fascinating information that he had a conviction for grievous bodily harm. Before becoming a Christian, he had been violently opposed to the Merseyside invasion of the best holiday property sites on the north Wales coast and, indeed, I suspect he had been involved in illegal acts, such as burning holiday homes, but I was assured that he was a reformed character.

We found various ways to cooperate and we printed a significant quantity of Welsh language material for schools and church activities.

## Frontier Youth Trust

The Reverend David Shepherd was famous for several things, not least his skill as a cricketer in a way that qualified him for sporting heroism. He had played cricket for England but gave up under the pressures of his work in the east end of London. However, it came to pass that England took a real hammering in one Ashes series against Australia and Reverend David was called back to the England team, despite his lack of recent practice. Inevitably, in a way that not even the Wizard or the Hotspur would have had the cheek to write, he scored a century on his first return.

However, fame alone was not enough to grapple with the deprivation and discouragement among young people of the East End. With Michael Eastman, another warrior against the deprivation of east London, he started a youth organisation called Frontier Youth Trust and he asked Scripture Union to act as a kind of big brother with administration. It was a messy arrangement which produced irritation on both sides, as I had seen from a distance when living in Scotland.

Shortly after moving to SU HQ in Milton Keynes, I had a meeting with Michael which went exactly like this.

ME    Peter I think FYT needs to be a separate organisation from SU.

PK    I absolutely agree.

ME    You agree?

PK    Yes. We will give you a departing gift of £xxx and you will be entirely at liberty to run your own affairs without reference to us again.

ME    Oh, hang on a minute! We would still want you to deal with admin and staff salaries. You keep that, but leave us to be independent on all other matters.

PK    No! Independence means just that. You are all grown up.

There were two interesting sequels to that. The FYT Treasurer was a real East End man and called me a name beginning with letter B that is OK in that part of London but unusual in SU circles. But to my surprise he had the grace to say, some months later, that it was the best thing that had happened to FYT. They had grown up.

I remember chance phone calls and letters from strange places. One letter was from a Nigerian man who wrote from a Japanese prison, asking me to send some Bible-reading material. He had come to faith at school in Nigeria but fell in with drug dealers and, eventually, to the jail in Japan. The prodigal was starting to make his way home.

Another was a Nigerian doctor who was tremendously excited that SU was thinking of starting behind the old Iron Curtain. He was about to go Tajikistan to be married in Dushanbe, the capital, where his fiancée lived. I asked the obvious question: What were you, a Nigerian, doing in Dushanbe? In the old Soviet days he had been awarded a scholarship to study medicine and while there he had found a wife.

That was the beginning of an SU relationship which continues to this day. I travelled far and wide as a visiting preacher in many churches but one church in Bristol sticks in the memory. The gist of the sermon was that responsible parents would not leave their children without any guidance about road safety, reasonably good dietary habits and healthy living, so too with learning about the God who made them. Human beings are not the products of blind chance; matters of right and wrong are not arbitrary subjective judgements. There are eternal truths in God's word which we ignore at our peril. I have never known so many people who thanked me and urged me to keep going.

## Beach Missions: Greystones, Republic of Ireland

As mentioned elsewhere, SU began on a beach – at Llandudno, to be precise – and that has continued since then. I visited three of them in my time in with SU England and one in particular gave me particular pleasure. It was at Greystones, Co. Wicklow in the Republic of Ireland, a place that brings back golden memories of childhood. During the War, my family lived in Northern Ireland which was subject to the same regime of food rationing as the rest of Britain, so our summer holidays were always on a farm in the Republic – where food was abundant and unrationed. The first boiled egg was a celebration, particularly since it was laid by a known and named hen. The farm where we stayed – Old Fort – had a horse, three cows and an assortment of fowl and a small number of fields for harvesting with a horse-drawn binder. If heaven is like that, bring it on.

Leap forward to the summer of 1999 and I was invited to be part of the summer mission on the golden beach. I asked about the involvement of the local churches and the story went like this.

> Well, there are five churches in the local area: Brethren, Baptist, Presbyterian. Anglican and Roman Catholic. In years gone by we could perm three out of five: either Brethren, Baptist and Presbyterian or Presbyterian, Anglican and Catholic. But for the past few years all five have joined together and that is how it is now. Thank God!

Three cheers for ecumenism! There is something wonderfully Irish about it and enormously encouraging. SU had an excellent outdoor centre with a large turnover of young people coming for outdoor holidays and events. The Director of the Centre described himself as an Evangelical Catholic, God bless him!

I visited Port St Mary on the Isle of Man and Southwold on the east coast of England when they had their centenaries. Perhaps the most memorable one was in Criccieth, Wales because Songs of Praise on the beach was recorded from it.

Sadly, SU Wales does not yet exist, but SUEW has an established Welsh staff team (Welsh living, Welsh speaking) with local initiatives and groups coming into partnerships in mission from across Wales. Development of Welsh language resources continues. Who knows what the future holds?

## International Councils

As previously mentioned, my introduction to the international work of SU came in 1984 at the first such event in Zimbabwe, when there was a vision for planting SU in the Communist countries of eastern Europe. There was a second council in Maastricht in 1991 at which we had the first Russian visitors. John Simmons, the Chairman of SU England, was very keen to celebrate the new millennium by having a third International Council which would have members from new movements behind what had been the Iron Curtain. To avoid the Millennium, it was held in 2001.

Nottingham University was the chosen venue. It had a good auditorium and accommodation at reasonable prices so invitations went out to all our national movements and a few that did not appear on our list of members, since they were in countries hostile to Christian churches or movements. In all, we had representatives from 110 countries, if I remember rightly and simultaneous translation in at least four languages. At the last moment we were able to add impromptu Russian for delegates.

It was a particular joy to have representatives from Latvia, Ukraine, Czechoslovakia, Armenia and Romania from behind the now-vanished Iron Curtain. The conference ended just before the 9/11 disaster, so much so that some of our delegates had difficulty getting home.

It was also a personal joy for me since it was the latest stage, but not the last, of a journey with Scripture Union which began with Cecil Johnson and his game of puddox in the grounds of Lushington Hall in Ooty in 1948. Or so I thought until someone asked me about a beach mission in Northern Ireland, and I remembered that I was a daily customer for the Beach Mission in Ballyholme Bay – aged five.

# 8 Retirement

Moving house is a chore and a thrill. We had to be in the Edinburgh area but that included many possibilities. While I wound up matters in Milton Keynes, Hilda house hunted with the help of our friend Julie Taylor. They identified eleven possibilities and after the tenth Hilda said, "No more!" Fortunately, Julie bullied her into the twelve miles or so to Dirleton, where we hope to live happily ever after.

There has been a village in Dirleton since the Iron Age. It has a triangular village green on which witches have been burned; a thirteenth century castle on a very solid lump of rock; a church built in 1614 C.E., the year after the publication of the King James Version of the Bible; The Castle Inn, the Open Arms Hotel and some six hundred very fortunate inhabitants. Rose Cottage was probably about three hundred years old with a long narrow garden in desperate need of loving attention. What could be better? We bought it.

Hilda and I sit lightly to ecclesiology. We prefer to worship locally; we look for churches that show signs of life and growth and we can live with denominational differences. So, we have in our married life been in Brethren, Episcopal and Presbyterian Churches to our great benefit. We have been very happy members of Dirleton Kirk, which is three minutes' walk from our first home. Revd David Graham has been our Minister, and Hilda was Session Clerk for six years.

I will always be grateful for my Brethren background for it gave me a thorough knowledge of the Bible and taught me that, like every other human being, I am made by God and for God and that God may be known in my own experience through the life, death and resurrection of Jesus.

My five years at an Anglican boarding school gave me a great respect for the Anglican form of worship which I shall always appreciate. Five years of singing in a choir have left a deposit of great words and hymns which will be with me for the rest of my life.

My twenty and more years as a Presbyterian made me aware that the Church is for the whole community for which we have a living responsibility. I will always be grateful for the Wednesday prayer meeting in Dirleton Kirk, which has been going for over thirty years.

## The Church and the Churches

Throughout life we are constantly reacting to our history and this is particularly true at present. Many churches in Scotland were built in the nineteenth century to meet the spiritual needs of people in scattered rural communities and they needed to be within walking distance of the population they served. Some have remarkable histories, but now many are redundant, either because attendance has declined or the easy accessibility of the digital age means that people can 'attend' worship from their own homes. What is to be done with the buildings?

Since retirement in 2001 I have been drawn into Pulpit Supply and Locum work in at least thirty-one rural and town Churches of Scotland. In Appendix 2, I have listed all the churches where I have done Locums or Pulpit Supply and each has particular memories.

Like many good things in life, it came about quite by chance when I did a pulpit supply in Humbie at the request of the longest-serving Session Clerk in the Kirk, Donald Hardy. Humbie was one of four churches which were served by a single minister.

I filled the gap during a lengthy vacancy, but as time passed without a permanent appointment, I asked the Interim Moderator if he could he find a locum in the interest of continuity. The answer was, "No, I can't find a locum so would you do it?" and that is what happened.

The first funeral I took was memorable. A young man who lived a wild life of raves, drinking bouts and motor bike accidents, eventually killed himself and I went to visit his parents. As I left, I asked if it would be a big funeral. The answer was, "No, my husband and I will be the only ones. He had no friends round here."

She could not have been more wrong. The funeral parlour was packed with many people standing. It was a testament to the young man's mother who, time and again, had met him from prison, cleaned him up and fed him, for it all to fall apart again.

I also took the funerals of three centenarians – all of them women!

East Saltoun will live long in my memory for an unfortunate event during a funeral service. It was a particularly windy day and we were singing the final hymn before moving to the Kirk yard for the interment, when suddenly the ceiling fell down on two unfortunate ladies in the back row. I completed the burial and returned to the kirk at the same time as the police and not one fire brigade but two, plus an ambulance. I gather that the person who called the emergency services said that the ceiling had collapsed, which was true up to a point, but ninety-five percent of it remained intact. Fortunately, the injuries were fairly minor and first aid was applied without the need for a trip to hospital. In fact, there was an air of disappointment about the fire brigade who were itching to do heroic things. However, it was comforting to know that the emergency services are eager and ready to serve, even when unnecessary.

It is fairly standard for many ministers to do two consecutive services on a Sunday and that was the case in a brief Locum I did at Belhaven and Spott. The outgoing minister left behind an appreciative congregation in a well-filled church on a Sunday morning. Some people have a gift for providing a children's item in the service before they scatter to their other activities, but I always found that the most difficult thing to prepare. I was saved by our dog Badger, and over time he chased ducks in the river Tweed and nearly drowned; had an expensive sore ear; was disobedient; tried to fly like a bird; mourned for my wife while she was in hospital for a week and had a resurrection day experience when she finally returned home – and many more.

Spott was a pleasure of a different kind and it was typical of many, small rural congregations. Although it was only two miles or so from Belhaven, the congregation was very united in their commitment to the church and the village. They were also tolerant of my idiosyncrasies. As the Church of Scotland rationalises by closing and merging congregations, Spott is due to close and the same is true of many like it all over the country where social change and other factors have made buildings redundant.

What will happen to the 'church' namely the congregation? Some will travel to Belhaven but not all, including the elderly. The building will be sold, and the Kirk's financial situation will be temporarily relieved and then what? Has the Kirk got a vision for revival and new growth? "Without a vision the people perish."

Then the Covid lockdown made church services difficult or impossible. Many people who previously came to church preferred to participate online, but thereby lost the reality of being a congregation. This change has come to stay. But the opposite has also happened. People who either did not use online services or did not like them, have come back and the post-service coffee in our church hall is a very noisy and convivial gathering.

I look back with great affection to almost a year at Penicuik North congregation. They were very indulgent about my deficiencies. My first funeral was a memorable one, because the deceased was a very popular figure in the town, having been the receptionist at the medical practice and later the manager of the community centre so every seat was filled, including the balcony, and there were many standing. In discussing the service with the family they were very distressed and we gathered stories that illustrated her popularity in the community, but each story seemed to provoke more distress, so I asked for and got a happy one to close with.

There had been a family picnic and a happy day out. Father had, for the first time, bought a pair of glasses en route, so mother said, "Let's have a look at your glasses", and father obliged. When he put them on, he said, "You know this! If I had had these glasses thirty years ago, I would never have married you."

I have happy memories of all the churches I served for various individual reasons. Stenton has recurring memories and one, in particular, had far-reaching consequences.

A good many years ago Dirleton Kirk formed a link with the MacFarlane Memorial Church in Kalimpong, North India, with fraternal visits in both directions. Agriculture in the foothills of the Himalayas is difficult, but an attempt was made to raise pigs with the help of a well-known pig breeder near Stenton who kindly offered to show our visitors how pigs are reared in Scotland. To say that our visitors were astonished at the rows and rows of vast sows lying prostrate on the floor while a regiment of piglets guzzled at their udders is an under-statement. The idea of thousands of pigs being bred in a year was beyond them, but they had been promised artificial insemination for a boar, since they had started in a small way.

"How many sows have you got?" they were asked.

"Two."

They accepted the kind offer, and indeed this had some initial success, but sadly various types of swine fever circulate unchecked in India. There seems little prospect of future success.

Stenton church is memorable for many reasons, not least the congregation and the music. Stenton, like Dirleton, enjoyed the generosity of Lady Elgin or Lady Mary Hamilton Nisbet, to use her first name. In Dirleton she paid for a bell tower and a wall to be erected round our castle. and she also paid for the building of Stenton church. Hers is an interesting story and indeed it will run and run until Lord Elgin returns his marbles (I mean that in the original sense and not the slang) to Greece – if ever.

**And Finally!**

I thank God for many things – in chronological order:

First, for my parents who took with total seriousness Jesus' call to "seek first the Kingdom of God" and they did indeed find that countless blessings followed from that.

Second, for my brother Ashley and sisters Carol and Joyce who indulged and supported their kid brother far beyond the call of duty.

Third, for Cecil Johnson and the place that the Bible and Scripture Union have had in my life.

Fourth, for Hilda, my wife, who against all advice from some who knew me well, risked it and married me anyway.

Finally for my sons, Ashley and Barry, and their wives Kerry and Cele, and their children Cameron, Rory, Maisie and Erin, and Archie and Dougal.

# Appendix 1

(Note: many of the errors of spelling and punctuation are retained, though a few improvements have been made to make the report readable!)

REPORT OF JOURNEY MADE FROM THE ARGENTINE IslandS
27th Aug. to 7th Sept., 1963
BY R LEWIS
with illustrations by P.R. Blakeley and C P Kimber

Extract from Journey Book:

Proposed to investigate Mt. Balch – Mt. Peary region from a fixed camp east of Il t -MI 11 on foot. and on skis.[t]

The purpose of the journey was mainly recreational though it was hoped to determine finally the possibility of a route onto the Plateau from the Bussey Glacier.

PREPARATORY JOURNEY

On August 22nd, the Party, P.R Blakeley, C.P. KImber and R. Lewis assisted by T.Talliß left Base with a dog team to establish the camp behind 11t.Æill. A previous depot journey had taken food and paraffin onto the Mt.Mill col. The sledge carried about .400lbs. of equipment and the load was relayed up the Ramp at Cape Rasmussen. The snow surface was very bad and only a further mile and a half was covered before camp was pitched.

On the following day the load was relayed in deep quite feasible soft snow onto the Col in bad visibility and together with the depot left there earlier was taken down to the intended camp site. The party returned to Base in extremely bad visibility, having left the tent adequately storm guyed and equipment suitably stored. The sea—ice in Penola (strait) was in good condition apart from a few thin patches near the Yalour Islande.

## ACCOUNT OF MAIN JOURNEY

On the 27th. the weather improved and it was possible to leave Base early, and over to the Camp.

The day was cold and clear and the tent and equipment were found in good order.

Aug. 28th. The weather had become overcast during the night but visibility below 3000 $^t$ was quite reasonable. Set off to reconnoitre the route towards Mount-Balch leaving the skis after an hour and climbing in deep soft snow to a col at 11100 $^t$ After crossing the col reached 2000' on a grnall glacier below a ridge from Balch before returning to Camp in deteriorating weather. An aneroid barometer was set at Camp (700 $^t$) each morning and readings were later corrected assuming linear change in sea—level pressure during the day.

Aug. 29th. More or less complete white—out conditions and so, the Primus wasn't working too well, it was decided to fetch the one from the Rasmussen Depot. The first attempt to reach Rasmussen failed due to atrocious visibility but later in the day the second attempt was more successful.

Aux. 30th.    A clear cold day and the route of the 28$^{th}$ was followed onto the  Mt.Balch ridge. Deep soft snow made progress arduous but no casualties were encountered in finding a route through crevasses and so onto the ridge. A step on the ridge at about 3000}' 3000'/ necessitated some climbing which was very pleasant. It was not possible to reach the summit of Balch due to lack of time and return was made from a significant snow dome on the ridge at 3550' .

Aug. 31st. Another fine day with the temperature again well below —20 $^0$ 0. The morning was spent drying out clothes and in the afternoon a route was worked out up the true right of the Bussey Glaciere A height of 2700 $^t$ was reached about five miles from Camp on the upper part of the glacier The view of the final ice—cliffs onto Peary made a route look quite feasible

Sept. 1st. Although the temperature wag still low shocking visibility necessitatecl lie—up e

Sept. 2nd. An early start was made in clear cold weather and the Bussey Glacier route of the 1st. was followed and then continued to 3150 f$^t$ at a distance eight miles from Camp after four hours skiing. Rather chill conditions were encountered the route being all the way in shadow, and as some extremities weren't getting any warmer it was decided advisable to return. Still the final slopes onto Peary looked possible and It was hoped to try again on a warmer day. Camp was reached three hours later at 9.pm. A determined effort was made to thaw out the boots that evening.

Sept. 3rd. Another cold day, this time in the sun and so the temperature , −29 °C midday at Base, didn't worry us and the summit at 11 t. Balch was reached. Skis were carried on an Everest frame over the small col and it was possible to make rapid progress over the glacier and onto the ridge where very deep soft conditions underfoot had caused delay on the 30th. Little time was lost in negotiating the steps and Mt. Balch was reached, 5 hours after leaving Camp , at The height was found to 3900 ᵗ and after taking numerous photographs and a round of' angles with the prismatic compass, all haste was made back to Camp where Pete's birthday was celebrated in high spirits.

This additional excerpt is included to illustrate the kind of work that was done to survey the area round base.

Aug. 28th. The weather had become overcast during the night but visibility below 3000 ᵗ was quite reasonable. Set off to reconnoitre the route towards IT t -Balch leaving the ski after an hour and climbing in deep soft snow to a col at 1110 ᵗ After crossing the col reached 2000' on a grnall glacier below a ridge from Balch before returning to Camp in deteriorating weathu. An aneroid barometer was set at Camp (700 ᵗ) each morning and readings were later corrected assuming linear change in sea—level pressure during the day.

Aug. 29th. More or less complete white—out conditions and so, the Primus wasn't working too well, it was decided to fetch the one from the Rasmussen Depot. The first attempt to rech Rasmussen failed due to atrocious visibility but later in the day the second attempt was more successful.

Aug. 30th. A clear cold day and the route of the 28th. was followed onto the Mt.Balch ridge. Deep soft snow made progress arduous but no difficulties were encountered in finding a route through crevasses and so onto the ridge. A step on the ridge at about 3000}' 3000'/ necessitated some climbing whlch was very pleasant. It was not possible to reach the summit of Balch due to lack of time and return was made from a significant snow dome on the ridge at 3550' •

<u>Aug 31st</u>. Another fine day with the temperature again well below −20 ° 0. The morning was spent drying out clothes and in the afternoon a route was worked out up the true right of the Bussey Glaciere A height of 2700 ' was reached about five miles from Camp on the upper part of the glacier The view of the final ice—cliffs onto Peary made a route look quite feasible.

<u>Sept. 1st</u>. Although the temperature wag still low shocking visibility necegsltatecl lie—up

<u>Sept. 2nd</u>. An early start wag made in clear cold weather and the Bussey Glacier route of the st. wag followed and then continued to 11500 ' at a distance eight miles from Camp after four hours skiing. Rather chill conditions were encountered ѕthe route being all the way in shadow, and ae some extremities weren't getting any warmer it was decided advisable to return. Still the final slopes onto Peary looked possible and It wag hoped to try again on a warmer day. Camp was reached three hours later at k.prn. A determined effort was made to thaw out the boots that evening.

<u>Sept. 3rd</u>. *Another cood day, this time in the sun and so the temperature −29 ⁰C midday at Base, didn't worry us and the summit o? Il t. Balch was reached. Skis were carried on an Everest frame over the small eol and it was possible to make rapid progress over the glacier and onto the ridge where very deep soft conditions underfoot had caused delay on the 30th. Little time was lost in necotiating the step and Mt. Balch was reached, 5 hours after leaving Camp , at The height was found to 3900 ' and after taking numerous photographs end round of' angles with the prismatic compass, all haste was made back to Camp where Pete's birthday was celebrated in high spirits.*

# Appendix 2

To the best of my recollection, I have done Pulpit Supply or Locum work at the following churches:

*Dirleton, Aberlady, North Berwick St Andrew Blackadder, Pencaitland, Ormiston, Gifford, Bolton, Saltoun, Humbie, Prestonpans, Port Seton, Dalkeith St Nicholas Buccleuch,, Bonnyrigg, Gorebridge, Penicuik North, Penicuik South, Howgate, Penicuk St Mungo's, West Linton, Fala, Traprain, Borthwick, Garvald, Moreham, Stenton, Whitekirk, Athelstaneford, Belhaven, Spot, Dunbar Parish, Haddington St Mary's.*